FAST EASY CHEAP vegan

FAST EASY CHEAP *vegan*

101 RECIPES

30 >>> OR LESS
MINUTES

10 >>> OR LESS
INGREDIENTS

$10 >>> OR LESS

SAM TURNBULL

appetite

Appetite by Random House® and colophon are registered trademarks of Penguin Random House LLC.

Library and Archives Canada Cataloguing in Publication is available upon request.
ISBN: 9780525610854
eBook ISBN: 9780525610861

Cover and book photography: Sam Turnbull
Printed and bound in China

Published in Canada by Appetite by Random House®,
a division of Penguin Random House Canada Limited.

www.penguinrandomhouse.ca

10   9   8   7   6   5   4   3   2

appetite
by RANDOM HOUSE

Penguin
Random House
Canada

This book is dedicated to my sister, Emma, who is the shining example of how to approach life with strength, tenacity, and endless warmth! Thank you for being the amazing inspiration that you are.

CONTENTS

HI, FRIENDS!

Sam Turnbull here . . . and for the rest of the book for that matter. I'm in total awe of the love and support I've received over the years on my blog, YouTube channel, and social media, and with my first cookbook, *Fuss-Free Vegan*. When writing that book, my goal was to share my everyday comfort food favorites, veganized, to help make cooking plant-based food easier and more delicious. I wanted to take the "weird" out of vegan and to show people that eating a plant-only diet is really quite easy to do. You don't need to be a health nut or a master chef to make good food, and you don't even have to be vegan to enjoy a plant-based meal!

I'm thrilled that my book made it into so many kitchens, and I'm completely blown away by the hundreds of rave reviews it received online! I was touched every time someone shared a photo on social media of one of the dishes made in their own kitchen. My heart melted when I heard that *Fuss-Free Vegan* became a go-to resource for so many. And I turned into a complete puddle of mush when fans brought their tattered, stained, heavily dog-eared, and bookmarked copies of my book to signings—because, in my opinion, there's no better review for a cookbook than when it's well-worn. ☺

And now I'm excited to go on this adventure with you again with another cookbook that's jam-packed full of the best vegan eats! Oowee, are there ever a whole lot of good recipes in this book. Get your forks ready because if you liked my first book, it gets even quicker, easier, cheaper, and totally drool-worthy delicious. But first . . .

MY STORY

If you're new to me and my story, hello and welcome! Let me tell you a little about my journey and how I got here.

I'm the last person in the world I thought would go vegan. Before you disagree and point me out as a girl who looks like she has always been veg, hear me out. I grew up an avid meat eater. There were animal heads on the walls of my family's house. I used to go fishing for fun, and I liked my steaks rare and bloody. No joke.

It weirds me out a little to share this with you now, but I think it's important to be honest. We all start somewhere. Whether your goal is to go full-on vegan (yay!) or just to reduce animal-product consumption (awesome!), every bit helps; I support you. No matter where you are on your path toward veganism, it's A-OK. Every action we take makes a difference no matter how small, and I applaud that. It's *so* much better to do something than to do nothing at all. So congratulate yourself for the changes you've made so far—like getting your hands on a copy of this book!

When I went vegan in 2012, I took the extreme route and changed overnight. All it took for me were a couple of documentaries and—boom!—no meat on my plate ever again. But I admit, it was difficult. At the time, "vegan" was still a word I had to explain to almost every friend and family member, and definitely every restaurant server. While some vegan products were available in stores, they were difficult to find, expensive, and, really, just not that great tasting. It was nothing compared to the latest plant-based-products craze that's going on these days, with all of these cool vegan options popping up in every grocery store, restaurant, and fast-food chain.

Honestly, though, I'm not complaining. If good vegan eats had been easier to find back then, maybe I wouldn't have felt the need to create my own recipes, and maybe my blog *It Doesn't Taste Like Chicken* would never have come to fruition. And both of my cookbooks wouldn't exist either!

Those early days of plant-based eating forced me to be creative in the kitchen. If I wanted to truly enjoy my food, none of the health-focused, raw, dehydrated, brown mushy stuff or stick-to-the-roof-of-your-mouth vegan cheeses was going to do it for me. I craved hearty, satisfying foods that didn't feel like they were lacking anything. I wanted dishes that I could proudly share with my friends and family whether they were vegan or not. I didn't want to apologize for the lack of anything. So with these challenges in mind, I started developing my own recipes. But I have a secret . . .

I'M NOT A CHEF

I'm not a trained chef. I didn't go to culinary school, I've never worked in a professional kitchen, I wasn't taught fancy knife skills, and my only experience working in a restaurant was busing tables (which I soon learned I hated and quit after only three days). In fact, I never even refer to myself as a chef, as the word in French directly translates to "chief," and I'm not the chief of anyone—I'm the only person in my kitchen!

This is good news. The benefit of never being professionally trained is that when it comes to developing recipes, I don't feel limited by the "rules" of cooking. I have no problem using ingredients in ways that aren't traditional. I feel creatively free to make up recipes that didn't exist before. I love taking on the challenges of adapting animal-product-filled recipes with substitutions that may not be standard. It always surprises me how many chefs feel that they are thinking out of the box by providing a salad or portobello burger as their vegan option. Really? Professionally trained, and that's all you've got up your sleeve?

Now don't get me wrong, I know many trained chefs, and many of them are awesomely creative. I absolutely love that so many restaurants have vegan options these days, but I also feel that sometimes we box ourselves in. Anyone can learn to color within the lines, but it's those who are brave enough to color outside the lines who are going to make changes. And lucky for you, I *am* professionally trained as an artist, and I love to color outside the lines—both in my art and with my cooking.

Lentils in Korean food? Not traditional at all, but lentils make an amazing ground beef substitute, and when infused with Korean-inspired flavors, give you a delicious, healthy, quick-to-make dinner (I recommend trying my Sweet Korean Lentils on page 182). Avocado in pasta? I had never even heard of serving avocado warm before going vegan, but when you blend ripe avocados with basil and other seasonings, they make for a quick, creamy, amazing pasta sauce that has become a go-to staple in my house (check out Presto Avocado Pesto on page 150).

Just as I have no problem combining ingredients that may not be traditional, I'm also A-OK with cheating along the way to make recipes easier and quicker to whip up. Caramelized onions may traditionally take an hour or longer to prepare, but I figured out a 10-minute hack that works, and I love it (see Cheater Caramelized Onion Pasta on page 157). Make-ahead mixes? You better believe I'm all for their ease and convenience (learn more on pages 27–48). Cheap grub? I'm all about it. I don't think food has to be expensive or require rare ingredients to be interesting or delicious.

So if I'm not a chef, then what am I? I like to refer to myself as a home cook, and in my opinion that's a great thing, because guess what, if you plan on prepping your dinner in your kitchen at home and not in a professional kitchen, then you too are a home cook! My recipes have been developed for the home, not for the restaurant. You don't need a chef's coat or funny poufy white hat. I'm here to tell you that you don't need super industrial-style kitchen equipment, fancy knife skills, or years of training to make good food. From one home cook to another, if I can do it, you can do it too.

WHY FAST EASY CHEAP VEGAN?

I've heard the complaints before: a vegan diet is too time-consuming, too much work, and too expensive! But what if I told you that that's all wrong? That cooking homemade plant-based meals can actually be quick. Like really quick. Like 30 minutes or less kind of quick. And what if I told you that these 30-minutes-or-less meals could be easy to prepare with just a few steps and with a maximum of 10 ingredients in each recipe? And what if I told you that all of these super fast and simple dishes could be quite cheap while you're at it? I'm talking $10 or less for the entire recipe. Sound too good to be true? Well it's not. I'm telling you! I even wrote a whole book about it, and you're holding it now!

So why is it that so many people think plant-based food is difficult and costly? Well, because it often is. Sometimes. Hear me out. There are definitely many vegan recipes that require hard-to-find and overpriced ingredients. It could be fancy schmancy superfoods from costly health-food stores, or it could be processed junk food from the freezer section. Either way, there are some seriously expensive products out there clearly labeled with a big *V* for vegan. Don't get me wrong, I love many of these foods. The more vegan options, the better, in my opinion, but if blowing your paycheck on a package of un-chicken isn't your idea of a good time, then you don't have to do it.

Every single grocery store already is filled to the brim with very affordable and totally delicious (when prepared correctly) vegan foods. I'm talking vegetables, fruits, grains, beans, nuts, seeds, and spices! Most of these won't have any kind of fancy vegan label on them, and they don't need to because this is the basis of what vegan food is. Compare any piece of meat (or even a processed vegan product) to the price of a can of beans and the beans will win in cost almost every time. Bonus points: beans are so much healthier for you too.

OK, so you get it, plant-based food is available and affordable, but if you're thinking that making food from scratch is *so* difficult and time-consuming, you're correct again . . . if you're trying to create some serious Michelin-star recipes. But I take it you aren't. Heck, I'm not even trying to do anything like that, and I develop recipes for a living. If there's one thing I've learned over the years, it's that most of us just want simple, quick, and delicious food that we can either dive into by our lonesome or serve with confidence to our friends and family.

Complicated recipes can be fun once in a while, but generally our weekdays don't need any more challenges than they're already filled with, and I personally like to make my weekends as challenge-less as possible. So I spent all the time and effort testing recipe after recipe to fill this book with dishes that are truly stress-free, accessible, quick, totally hearty, and delicious, so that you can spend more time doing the things you love—like eating!

This book is for the busy parent, the stressed nine-to-fiver, the overloaded student, or the better-things-to-do-than-cook type of person. Through this book, I will show you that having a full plate can take on a whole new meaning!

HOW THIS BOOK WORKS

All of the recipes in this book cost $10 or less to prepare, require 10 ingredients or less, and take 30 minutes or less to put together. Every single recipe! Pretty cool, right?

There are a few things to note:

For the ingredients, I considered salt, black pepper, olive oil, and a light oil (such as canola or vegetable) to be kitchen staples. This means that I didn't include them as part of the 10 ingredients. I did include them in the cost, however. Every other ingredient, including veggies, fruits, specialty oils, beans, legumes, nuts, seeds, or other spices are counted as one of the 10 ingredients.

That said, I admit that I've cheated a little. Spices are my favorite ingredients and, in my opinion, are the ultimate secret to great food. To avoid an endless list of spices, and to avoid bland food (no thank you!), throughout the book I took advantage of using spice mixes. All the spice mixes I used should be readily available in your grocery store, but I've also included recipes for your own homemade versions of these mixes. If you already have a large cabinet of spices, head to page 48 to start whipping up your own blends. Or if you're lazy (no judgment from me), just buy the premade versions. Either way, these blends will do most of the work for you and make your food taste super delicious with just a spoonful.

For the pricing, I wanted to make 100 percent sure that each one of these recipes cost $10 or less to prepare, and the only way to do that was to price them out to ⅛ teaspoon. Food prices ebb and flow and will change based on the brand you are buying, the store you are shopping at, the area you live in, and the season, so instead of listing the exact price of each recipe, I rounded up to either $1, $3, $5, $7, or $10. Please note that the prices in the book may not be exactly the same for you, but they should give you a pretty good idea.

To price the recipes, I looked at my local grocery store for the cost of each item (and my grocery store isn't a discount store). When pricing, I mostly stuck to generic brands because basic ingredients (which is what most of my recipes call for) generally don't vary much in taste or quality from brand to brand. So stop paying for the pretty packaging! Of course, I considered the more expensive items when budgeting, such as nuts, veggies (who knew red bell peppers were so expensive!?!), and fruits, but I also made sure to add up every tiny little detail. I actually took the time to figure out the price of ¼ teaspoon of cayenne (3 cents) and 3 tablespoons of all-purpose flour (also 3 cents), and I even counted how many peeled cloves of garlic were in the bulk bag I purchased (61, in case you were wondering). I was detailed with a capital D, and I always, always rounded up. I did all of this because I wanted to prove undisputedly that the recipes in this book really can cost just $10 or less and still be fantastic and easy to prepare.

Here's a fun story: When I started recipe testing for this book, I really didn't worry about the cost of things. I wasn't up for the math at that moment, so I put it off to figure it out later. It was only when I'd written the entire book that I decided to actually start pricing the recipes. Guess what happened? Almost every single recipe was already $10 or less. In fact, a ton of them were only about $5! I had to revise just a few recipes (mainly due to those pesky red bell peppers), but the majority of the book was good to go! The lesson? Cooking vegan is already so affordable when you cook from scratch.

Not only do I like to keep my meals affordable, but I'm the kinda girl who makes the mistake of starting to cook dinner when I'm already hungry. I know how to get dinner on the table in lightning speed from years of that going-to-faint-I'm-so-hungry experience. As a full-time recipe developer, I spend most days in the kitchen, so I may be a little quicker than you at chopping veggies or whisking up sauces, but I tried to be very fair with my timing, adding extra minutes when I thought the average home cook might take a little longer at a task. Get ready to have simple, scrumptious, plant-based recipes on the table in no time.

As you flip through the pages of this book, you'll see several icons, which indicate some helpful features each recipe offers. Here's what each icon means.

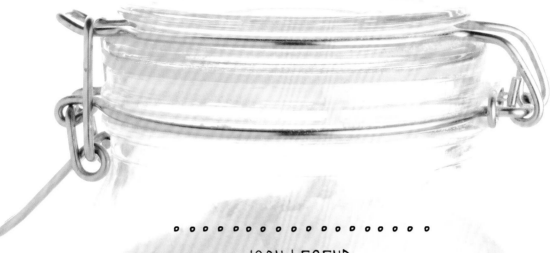

ICON LEGEND

ONE POT
This recipe requires only one pot to make the dish. Yay for fewer dirty dishes!

MAKE-AHEAD
Part of or the entire recipe can be made ahead of time. Cook now so you can save time later.

FREEZER-FRIENDLY
This recipe freezes well and can be thawed and reheated when ready to enjoy.

GLUTEN-FREE
This recipe is gluten-free or has the option to be made gluten-free.

CHOOSE YOUR OWN ADVENTURE
In this recipe you may choose from a selection of ingredients. This allows you to customize the recipe to your own taste preference or cook with the ingredients you already have on hand. Fewer trips to the store!

HOW TO COOK FAST EASY CHEAP VEGAN

Don't be intimidated by the kitchen. I've been cooking since before I can remember, and if wee-little-kid-standing-on-a-stool Sam can do it, I know you can do it too. Just because a chef may charge you some serious dough for a plate of pasta (you better believe that pun was intended), it doesn't mean that the pasta was actually difficult, super time-consuming, or even expensive to make. Preparing a good dish is mostly about complementary flavors and textures, and I already did all that hard work for you by writing this book. Now all you have to do is follow the instructions and get your fork ready.

To make things a breeze, here are my bonus tips on how to make cooking faster, easier, and cheaper.

FASTER

Roll up your sleeves because when I say go, I mean it! If you want to get out the door as soon as possible or catch your favorite reality TV show live, then here are my tips for speeding up the cooking process.

1. Give cooking your full attention. If you really want to get dinner on the table quick, you need to focus. So turn off the telly or other distractions, crack open this book, and get ready to cook! On the other hand, if you're not in a rush and you would prefer leisurely cooking, by all means, pour yourself a glass of wine, turn on some tunes, and cook at your own pace.

2. Multitask. Some recipes require an oven to preheat, a pot of water to boil, or grains to cook. Get these things going right away (they will always be step 1 in the instructions). Once they are going, start any prep work like chopping veggies or measuring ingredients, and begin any other cooking. I've become such a quick cook that I often have the entire meal prepped before the oven has even finished preheating! You'll get there too!

3. Get your tools ready. Depending on the recipe, you may need to use a blender or food processor, bowls, pots, skillets, stirring spoons, whisks, or a cutting board and knife. Collect the tools you need and have them ready to go. No last-minute looking for the blender lid!

4. Gather your ingredients. Use a tray or large baking sheet to round up all your ingredients. This will save you several trips to the pantry or digging through the back of the fridge to find that one carrot you swore you had. Having everything at hand will make prep work go super quickly.

5. Use a compost bowl or bin. Instead of cleaning up scraps and running all over the kitchen with them, have a bowl or bin within reach so you can toss the scraps as you go. I find it handy to put my green bin in a drawer under the counter right by my working space. This way I can just pull open the drawer and wipe scraps straight into the bin.

6. Chop small. I give you guidance for what size the veggies should be chopped for best texture, but if you want to speed up your cooking even more, the smaller the veggies are chopped, the faster they will cook. This is especially useful when making blended soups or sauces, since the veg is going to get mashed up anyway.

7. Opt for wider pans. When cooking on the stove, the more the food is able to spread out across the surface, the more contact it has with the hot pan and the faster it will cook. A smaller pot means the food is piled high with less direct contact, so it can take longer to cook. Also, the less food that is touching the bottom of the pan, the less browning will occur, and browning is a key to getting great flavor! This is why my large cast-iron skillet pretty much lives on my stovetop.

8. Use downtime to clean. If you are left with a little time while you wait for something to cook and there is nothing else to complete in the recipe, use this time to clean. I always feel doubly accomplished when dinner is finished and the kitchen is all cleaned up at the same time!

EASIER

Complicated doesn't mean better. In fact, I think it's the other way around. If a dish can be totally scrumptious *and* easy to prepare, it's the kind of recipe that you will come back to time and time again. The recipes in this book are written to be easy already, but here are some additional tips to help make cooking even more effortless.

1. Use good tools. I once saw a woman struggle to cut a carrot with a tiny dull knife. This horrific scene is the stuff of nightmares for me! If you are struggling with simple tasks in the kitchen, it's a good sign that you may be using the wrong tools. Make sure you use quality tools and keep them in peak condition. Keep those knives sharp, people! For tips on how to get your hands on some good equipment on a budget, see my Cheaper section (next page).

2. Get your prep on! It might seem efficient to chop veggies while the onions are sautéing, but if you're not a speedy chopper, you run the risk of burning the onions before the veggies are chopped and ready to add. Unless there is a lot of time between each step, such as roasting or boiling, it's easier to have all the ingredients prepped and ready to go so there are no last-minute stresses. If a bunch of ingredients are added to a recipe all at the same time, you can toss them all together into a large bowl to save room on your cutting board.

3. Read the recipe. Do you have a go-to recipe that feels so easy to prepare because you've made it a million times before? The same theory applies here. By reading the recipe, you will know what to do and what to expect, which will save you on last-minute stresses. The more you understand the recipe before you begin, the easier and quicker you will be able to prepare the dish.

4. Use proper measuring tools. Eyeballing ingredients may seem easy, but to get the best results, properly measuring is key. It's much easier to measure and have the recipe work out perfectly than to just eyeball the ingredients and wonder why things went wacky. This is especially true when baking, since that's just chemistry. Proper measurements ensure the recipe will work out the same way every time.

5. Stick to the recipe. It may be tempting to improvise or sub with what you have on hand, but changing a recipe will change the outcome of the dish, and not always for the better. Once you give the recipe a

try, you can always take notes and adjust it to your preference the next time around. Where possible, I include as many substitutions as I can in these recipes.

6. Roll with the punches. Recipe fail? I think not! Instead of getting upset, try renaming the dish. Accidently burn the cauliflower a little? Call it "charred cauliflower." Undercook the chocolate cake and it's a little gooey in the middle? Call it "chocolate pudding cake." Terrible plating skills? Call it "rustic." Sometimes all a dish needs is a new perspective to be a smash hit.

CHEAPER

Good food doesn't have to be expensive. Eating plant-based will already save you a ton of money, as meat and cheese are often the most expensive items on a grocery bill. But here are my tips to stretch your budget even further.

1. Skip the health-food stores. Health-food stores can be worth the splurge if you are looking for a fancy premade vegan product or a gluten-free alternative, but often they are just overpriced and a surefire way to blow your budget.

2. Buy local and in season. Not only does it taste way better, but it also is usually much cheaper since it doesn't have to be shipped in from faraway. If you buy in bulk, you can chop and freeze fruit and veggies to use later on.

3. Hit up the bulk-food stores. These are serious savers. Sure, some products might look cute in their fancy packaging, but you are likely paying a lot more for that. I find bulk stores are especially helpful for pricier items like spices and nutritional yeast. Plus, you can purchase the exact amount you need, which is super handy if you're experimenting with a new ingredient or shopping for a product you won't likely use again before it expires.

4. Plan ahead. Whenever I plan to go grocery shopping, I make a list of the recipes I intend to cook over the next week. Then I compare the ingredients lists with what I have in my cupboards and fridge. This saves me buying extra of things I don't need and prevents the need to run last-minute errands.

5. Don't buy processed foods. Sure, it can seem convenient to buy premade vegan specialty items, but these can add up quickly. Instead, use the recipes in this book to make your own versions at home.

6. Don't be tricked by pretty packaging. As someone who has worked in design, I'm a total sucker for a pretty label. But when you compare one can of chickpeas with said fancy label to another can with a boring label, the actual beans inside the can don't vary much. Keep in mind it's the end dish that matters, not how pretty your grocery cart looks.

7. Save on tools. Items like chef's knives and cast-iron pans can be found second-hand and easily restored at home. For tools such as food processors and blenders, see if you can get a hand-me-down or try having a look online at buy-and-sell sites to find deals on barely used or even new tools. These items also make for fantastic birthday, Christmas, or other gift requests.

8. Check your grocery store's website. My local store has a handy feature on their website that shows the cost for each item per 100 g or 100 mL, depending on the kind of product. This makes it super quick and easy to see which brands are actually the most affordable, regardless of how big or small the container is. I now like to reference this before heading to the store and jot down the brand I should buy so I don't have to try to calculate on the spot.

9. Keep those leftover liquids. Sun-dried tomatoes in oil, marinated artichokes, pickles, olives, capers, and canned pineapple in juice all have one thing in common: they come packed in awesome, flavor-infused liquids. Don't toss them out! Instead, try them in other dishes to add an instant boost.

10. Use what you already have. One of the worst wallet offenders is wasting the food you have already purchased. I made sure to include lots of recipes in this book that will help you use up the last bits of fruits, veggies, nuts, and any other random ingredients. Try my Grab & Blend Smoothie Kits (page 52), Toast Is the Most! (page 58), DIY Instant Oatmeal Packets (page 71), Mix 'n' Match Trail Mix (page 88), DIY Instant Ramen Soup (page 98), Tomato Sauce Amper-Uppers (page 152), Guzinta Bowls (page 190), Kitchen Sink Cookies (page 202), and Lickety-Split Ice Cream (page 216) for inspiration.

FAST EASY CHEAP VEGAN PANTRY

Be prepared to hunt for magic powders of wonder found only in the distant corner of the health-food store that is at least a 40-minute drive from your house. But don't worry, it will only cost you, well, everything. KIDDING! For the most part, the recipes in this book consist of ingredients you likely already know well, and can easily find at your local supermarket.

I provided a more in-depth fridge and pantry guide in my first book, *Fuss-Free Vegan*, but in case you don't have that book, I wanted to touch quickly on the most important ingredients and a few others that may be new to you.

PLANT-BASED MILKS

These days we are lucky that grocery store shelves are lined with all sorts of amazing plant-based milk options. Unless I'm specific in a recipe, use any kind you like, but I always recommend using an unsweetened plain version. So don't stir chocolate oat milk into your pasta—yuck! My favorite plant-based milk to cook with is an unsweetened soy milk, as it has a mild taste and a texture and fat content most similar to traditional dairy.

COCONUT MILK

For full-fat coconut milk, buy the kind in the can. Some cans of coconut milk can be watered down, making the milk way less creamy. Not good! Make sure to pick up a can that is higher in fat to avoid this. (Check out the can's nutrition label; my favorite brand to cook with has 11 g of fat per ⅓-cup serving.) High fat content makes it act more like a cream than a milk. If you wish to substitute for coconut milk, look for a plant-based milk that has a similar fat content for the best results. You could also blend 1 cup raw cashews with 1 cup water until completely smooth to make cashew cream, which works very well as a substitute for coconut milk.

VEGAN BUTTERS

Plant-based margarines and buttery spreads are readily available in grocery stores, either in the health-food section or sometimes right along with the other margarines. My go-to is Earth Balance Original Buttery Spread, which I find has the best texture for baking. If you need to substitute with something else, try coconut oil, but note that it won't have the same buttery taste and may make baked goods a bit greasy.

CHOCOLATE

Chocolate is made from the cacao bean, and as we know, vegans love beans. Dairy is often added to make milk chocolate or even many dark chocolates, so always check the ingredients to make sure the chocolate you are purchasing is vegan. You don't need to buy specialty brands; instead, try the baking or candy section of your grocery store for accidently vegan chocolate. My favorite chocolate to cook with happens to be the most affordable store brand that comes in an enormous bar. Very dangerous for the ease of snacking!

SWEETENERS

For liquid sweeteners, I like using corn syrup (which is very affordable), agave syrup, or maple syrup. Depending on where you live, white sugar and brown sugar may have been processed using bone char, which means they aren't vegan. Check the brand you are purchasing online or reach out to the brand for information. Or, if in doubt, buy organic sugar, which is always vegan. Here in Canada I use Redpath brand, which clearly states on its website that it is vegan-friendly.

OILS

Olive oil and lighter oils, such as canola and vegetable, are basic ingredients that you should always have on hand. Sesame oil is fantastic for adding a flavor boost to Asian-inspired dishes.

VINEGARS AND CITRUS

I use both of these for amazing flavor and to help some baked goods rise, such as my pancakes (page 28). Don't toss the peels of your citrus. Before you slice the fruit, use a zester or grater to gently scratch the zest from the fruit to add to dishes such as my 10-Ingredient Lemon Cream Pasta (page 158) and my Citrus & Coconut Custard Cups (page 205). My go-tos in this category are apple cider vinegar, lemons, and limes.

BLACK SALT

Also called kala namak, this salt tastes like eggs. No, really—it's the weirdest thing. Despite the name, the salt is actually pink and has a slight sulfur smell. If you want to make something taste like eggs, such as my Tofu Scramble (page 27), I highly recommend picking this up at an Indian grocery store or ordering it online. It's fairly inexpensive and a little goes a long way.

SPICES AND DRIED HERBS

Spices are the absolute key to great food. Salt and black pepper are basics you probably already have on hand, so now it's time to start expanding that spice cabinet! Buy spice mixes or make your own (page 48) to add a ton of flavor in one sprinkle.

FRESH HERBS

I love cilantro and parsley for fresh-flavor garnishes. I also use rosemary, thyme, sage, and mint in some of my recipes. In a pinch, if you are out of the fresh you can substitute dried at a three-to-one ratio. So, for example, if a recipe calls for 3 teaspoons fresh, you would use 1 teaspoon dried. That said, fresh herbs have a brighter flavor, so try to stick to fresh when called for in a recipe. I don't have a green thumb at all, but if you do, you could try growing your own herb garden.

CONDIMENTS

These are an excellent way of cramming a lot of flavor into recipes in one quick step. I love hot sauce, ketchup, barbecue sauce, soy sauce, Dijon mustard, pickles, capers, salsa, and vegan mayonnaise. Some barbecue sauces contain animal products, but many are already vegan, so double-check labels to be sure. Vegan mayonnaise is available in most grocery stores these days, but if you can't get your hands on some, mashed avocado makes a great healthy substitution (though it may make your food green).

NUTRITIONAL YEAST

This is the worst-named food ever, but this yellow flaky stuff is a vegan's secret weapon! It has an awesome cheesy taste and, bonus points, it's actually good for you. My local grocery store sells it but recently upped the price, so I prefer to buy it at bulk-food stores or order it online. I buy this stuff by the pound, and considering it weighs almost nothing, that means I always have lots on hand! If you're new to it, I recommend trying it several times before committing to a big bag. I didn't love the taste at first, but now I generously sprinkle it on popcorn!

LIQUID SMOKE

I know, it sounds creepy, but it's just the condensation collected from a fire. A few drops will instantly fill your dish with savory, smoky flavor. Find it in the barbecue sauce section in small bottles, usually on the top shelf. In a pinch, you can substitute with double the amount of smoked paprika.

SUN-DRIED TOMATOES

An all-time favorite ingredient of mine for their chewy, deep umami taste. The kind found in jars with oil are pricey, but the leftover oil can be used to make Pizza Popcorn (page 78) or in other tomato-based dishes such as pasta sauce or pizza. The sun-dried tomatoes that are dry, without oil, are more affordable, so I always have some on hand to add oomph to pastas, salads, or pizza.

ARTICHOKE HEARTS

You'll find marinated artichoke hearts in small jars by the sun-dried tomatoes. Use the leftover marinating liquid to enhance salad dressing (page 129–131), stretching your buck a bit further. Or you can find unmarinated artichoke hearts in water in cans. The artichokes in water are perfect for my 10-Minute Artichoke Salad Sandwiches (page 176).

WHITE MISO PASTE

Keep this on hand to add some umami and depth to dishes. You'll find it either on the shelf or refrigerated. Try it in a 5-minute miso soup with just some chopped tofu and sliced green onions, or get a bit more creative and make my 10-Minute Creamy Miso Udon Noodles (page 145).

TOFU

When done right, tofu isn't bland or boring. It's actually my favorite. (I know, how very vegan of me.) I use tofu of different firmnesses to get different textural results. When people ask why their tofu dish went wrong, it's often because they used the wrong firmness of tofu. It matters! Make sure you are using the required ingredients to get the best results.

BEANS, LEGUMES, AND LENTILS

Beans are cheapest when bought dry and cooked from scratch, but this takes a lot of time and forethought, so it's not really my thing. If you want to prepare your beans from scratch, by all means, go for it, but I prefer to go the canned route. My cupboard is always bursting with all kinds of beans— just drain and rinse and they are good to go! Red lentils, on the other hand, take only 10 minutes to prepare from scratch, so I generally purchase them dry. This way I can infuse them with a ton of flavor as they cook and absorb the liquid. Just be sure to keep them at a low simmer, and don't stir them too much to avoid them getting mushy. Brown or green lentils are fantastic as well, but they take twice as long as red lentils to cook, about 20 minutes.

GRAINS

I use white rice, quinoa, and couscous because these are all quick-cooking grains, but feel free to sub others that you enjoy. I'm also a fan of brown rice, but it takes a long time to cook (30 minutes or more), so it's not ideal for a quick meal.

FLOUR

I bake with regular old all-purpose flour for its great price and convenience. If you have a gluten sensitivity, you can try an all-purpose gluten-free blend. This should work seamlessly in recipes requiring only a small amount of flour, but in recipes such as my cakes, the results may vary a bit. I recommend using Bob's Red Mill Gluten Free 1 to 1 Baking Flour for the best results.

FROZEN FRUIT AND VEGETABLES

Don't be afraid of the freezer section. Frozen fruits and vegetables are frozen at peak ripeness, unlike the fresh fruit and veg that are usually picked underripe. I almost always have frozen corn kernels, edamame, peas, and fruit on hand.

MUSHROOMS

A favorite ingredient in the vegan world for their umami-packed flavor and meaty texture. There should be paper bags near the mushroom section of your grocery store, which is the best way to store them, as the bag allows them to breathe. (Sneaky tip: nab an extra bag and make DIY Microwave Popcorn on page 75.) Dried mushrooms can seem pricey, but they are chock-a-block full of amazing flavor. I use them in my Mushroom Gravy Mix (page 41), where a little goes a long way.

BREADS

Traditionally, bread is made with just flour, water, yeast, and salt—so totally vegan. These days, though, store-bought breads contain a long list of ingredients, sometimes including non-vegan ones. Always read the ingredients list to make sure the bread you are purchasing is vegan. As it takes me a while to get through an entire loaf of bread, I store mine in the freezer to keep it from spoiling. Just grab a frozen slice and let it thaw on your counter, or use it right away by tossing it in your toaster.

PASTA AND NOODLES

The dried pasta you find in the grocery store is usually vegan (just check the ingredients to be sure), whereas fresh pasta often contains eggs. Rice noodles are almost always vegan, whereas chow mein noodles may or may not contain eggs. It's always important to read the ingredients list, just to be sure. Feel free to play around with different noodle shapes and sizes!

NUTS AND SEEDS

Nuts like almonds, pistachios, hazelnuts, and cashews can be expensive, so I call for them sparingly in this book. Buying them in bulk makes them more affordable and you can purchase the exact amount you need. When I don't specify raw unseasoned nuts, use roasted and salted ones for some instant extra flavor. Sunflower seeds are very affordable, so I love using them to add some extra crunch for little cost. Quick tip: store nuts and seeds in the fridge or freezer to keep them fresher longer.

Now, on to the recipes!

Breakfast becomes easy peasy when you have a jar of this in your pantry! You can whip up a tofu scramble in minutes and enjoy it plain, or feel free to amp it up by first sautéing veggies, then adding beans or any garnishes you like. You can enjoy the scramble on toast, in a breakfast burrito, or in a bowl. The key to this spice mix is to use black salt (also called kala namak), which has an eggy taste. If you don't have access to black salt or don't want the eggy flavor, sub regular table salt to taste.

MAKES | About ½ cup seasoning, 4 batches tofu scramble

TOTAL TIME | 10 minutes

TOTAL COST FOR MIX | Under $3

COST PER PREPARED TOFU SCRAMBLE | Under $5

TOFU SCRAMBLE SEASONING

TO MAKE THE SEASONING

1. Add the nutritional yeast, black salt, onion powder, garlic powder, and turmeric to a sealable jar. Stir or shake well to combine. Store in your pantry for up to 2 years.

TO MAKE THE TOFU SCRAMBLE

1. Add the vegan butter or oil to a pan and heat. When hot, crumble your tofu of choice into the pan and sprinkle with 2 tablespoons seasoning. Stir to evenly distribute the seasoning and heat through, about 5 minutes.

QUICK TIP: Medium-firm tofu will result in a creamy and tender scramble, firm tofu will be a bit less tender, and extra-firm tofu is perfect for a drier scramble.

MAKE AHEAD: Prepared tofu scramble can be stored in an airtight container in the fridge for about 3 days. Enjoy cold or gently reheat in a pan or in the microwave.

FOR THE TOFU SCRAMBLE SEASONING

½ cup nutritional yeast

4 teaspoons black salt (also called kala namak)

3 teaspoons onion powder

1 teaspoon garlic powder

1 teaspoon turmeric

FOR THE TOFU SCRAMBLE (SERVES 4)

1 tablespoon vegan butter or oil

1 block (12–15 ounces) medium-firm, firm, or extra-firm tofu (see Quick Tip)

2 tablespoons Tofu Scramble Seasoning

MAKES | About 4½ cups mix, 3 batches pancakes or waffles (18–24 pancakes or 9–12 waffles)

TOTAL TIME | 15 minutes

TOTAL COST FOR MIX | Under $3

COST PER 1 BATCH PANCAKES/ WAFFLES | Under $3

Who doesn't love fluffy, gorgeous pancakes first thing in the morning? But who usually feels groggy and lazy and not in the mood to start measuring flour first thing in the morning? This girl. (Gestures both thumbs toward self.) Well, problem solved. Now I have a jar of this pancake and waffle mix ready to go to cut down on morning stresses. Serve your pancakes or waffles plain with vegan butter and syrup or try adding vanilla, spices, fruit, or even chocolate chips to the batter to amp them up a little.

PANCAKE & WAFFLE MIX

PANCAKE & WAFFLE MIX

4 cups all-purpose flour

⅓ cup white sugar

3 tablespoons baking powder

1 teaspoon salt

FOR THE PANCAKES OR WAFFLES
(MAKES 6-8 PANCAKES OR 3-4 WAFFLES)

1½ cups Pancake & Waffle Mix

1¼ cups plant-based milk, such as soy or oat

2½ tablespoons light oil, (such as canola or vegetable), plus more for frying

1 tablespoon lemon juice or apple cider vinegar

ADD-INS (OPTIONAL)

½ teaspoon vanilla extract

½ teaspoon cinnamon or Pumpkin Pie Spice (page 49 or store-bought)

½ cup berries, sliced bananas, chopped apples, or vegan chocolate chips

TO MAKE THE MIX

1. Add the flour, sugar, baking powder, and salt to a large jar, container, or sealable bag. Whisk or shake to combine, making sure everything is mixed well. Store in the airtight container at room temperature for up to 1 year.

TO MAKE THE PANCAKES OR WAFFLES

1. To a medium bowl, add 1½ cups pancake and waffle mix, plant-based milk, oil, and lemon juice. If you plan on adding vanilla or spices, add them now as well. Mix until everything comes together. Don't overmix the batter; lumps are totally fine (overmixing kills the bubbles, which are what make pancakes fluffy). If you are adding fruit or chocolate chips, gently fold them in once the batter is mixed.

2. For the pancakes: Heat a lightly oiled large skillet or non-stick frying pan over medium heat. When hot, use a ⅓-cup measure to scoop the batter into the pan, and use the edge of the cup to gently spread the batter to form a pancake. Cook for a couple of minutes, until large bubbles form on the surface and they are golden on the bottom. Gently flip the pancakes to cook on the remaining side for another 1–2 minutes, until golden. Repeat until all the batter is used up.

For the waffles: Heat your waffle iron, and when it's warmed, mist the iron with spray oil. Spoon about ⅔ cup of batter onto the iron and close. Allow to cook until the waffle is golden on each side. Use a fork to gently lift the waffle out of the iron. Repeat until all the batter is used up.

QUICK TIP: To keep pancakes or waffles warm, you can pile them in a heatproof dish in your oven set to 150°F to 200°F.

MAKE AHEAD: You can make these ahead of time and freeze prepared pancakes or waffles. Allow them to cool completely, spread in a single layer on a baking sheet, then freeze solid, about 2 hours. Store them in an airtight container or bag in the freezer for up to 2 months. Just pop them into your toaster to reheat.

MAKES | Just over 4 cups,
4 batches biscuits (24 biscuits)

TOTAL TIME | 25 minutes

TOTAL COST FOR MIX | Under $3

COST PER BATCH OF BISCUITS | Under $3

The best thing about making biscuits from scratch (apart from their deliciousness) is that basically the worse the dough looks—shaggy, falling apart, rough—the better the biscuits turn out! (Shaggy and rough = gorgeous fluffy layers.) Fresh biscuits served still warm from the oven are a great addition to almost any meal, but they go particularly well with my Mushroom Gravy (page 41), 30-Minute Minestrone (page 100), and Creamy Tuscan Mushrooms (page 185).

BISCUIT MIX

FOR THE BISCUIT MIX

4 cups all-purpose flour

3 tablespoons baking powder

2 teaspoons white sugar

1 teaspoon salt

FOR THE BISCUITS (MAKES 6)

1 cup Biscuit Mix

3 tablespoons cold vegan butter

¼ cup plant-based milk, such as soy or oat

1 teaspoon lemon juice or apple cider vinegar

QUICK TIP: Don't twist the cutter when cutting biscuits. This can seal the edges and will stop the biscuits from rising properly. Instead, just press the biscuit cutter straight down and pull straight up, gently wiggling (but not twisting) if needed.

TO MAKE THE MIX

1. Add the flour, baking powder, sugar, and salt to a large jar or sealable container. Whisk or shake well to combine, making sure ingredients are evenly distributed. Store in your pantry for up to 1 year.

TO MAKE THE BISCUITS

1. Preheat your oven to 450°F. Lightly grease a large baking sheet or line with parchment paper.

2. If using a food processor: Add 1 cup biscuit mix and the vegan butter, and pulse until the butter is incorporated and the mixture looks sandy. Add the plant-based milk and lemon juice and pulse just a few times until a shaggy dough forms but there is still lots of powder unmixed.

If making by hand: Cut the cold vegan butter into small cubes. Add 1 cup biscuit mix to a large bowl and scatter the butter cubes overtop. Use a pastry cutter or fork to cut the butter into the biscuit mix until you reach a sandy texture. Pour in the plant-based milk and lemon juice and mix until a shaggy dough forms but there is still unmixed flour in the bowl.

3. Dump the dough onto a clean work surface and use your hands to gently gather the dough and knead it just a few times until everything is incorporated. Gently pat the dough into a disk about ¾ inch thick. Use a 3-inch round cutter, a glass turned upside down, or a knife to cut biscuits (see Quick Tip). Collect the scraps and reform until you have used all the dough to make six biscuits.

4. Place the biscuits on the prepared baking sheet and bake for 8–10 minutes, until risen and golden on the bottoms.

MAKE AHEAD: You can bake these biscuits ahead of time and freeze them. Allow to cool completely, then toss in an airtight container or bag and freeze for 2–3 months. Allow biscuits to thaw at room temperature. Once the biscuits are thawed, you can warm them, if desired, by wrapping them in a damp paper towel and microwaving for 20–40 seconds.

Whether you like the kind of muffin that is basically just a chocolate chip cupcake with a healthier-sounding name, or you like an actually healthy whole wheat and fruit muffin, this mix is super customizable. Just decide whether you prefer using all-purpose, whole wheat, or a gluten-free flour blend and shake the mix up in a jar. Then, when ready to bake, choose your flavor add-ins—chocolate chips, fruit, or nuts!

MAKES | 5⅓ cups mix, 4 batches muffins (24 muffins)

TOTAL TIME | 25 minutes

TOTAL COST FOR MIX | Under $3

COST PER BATCH OF MUFFINS | Under $3 (not including add-ins)

MUFFIN MIX

FOR THE MUFFIN MIX

3½ cups all-purpose flour

1½ cups brown sugar or white sugar

2 teaspoons baking powder

2 teaspoons baking soda

1 teaspoon salt

FOR THE MUFFINS (MAKES 6)

1⅓ cups Muffin Mix

½ cup plant-based milk, such as soy or oat

¼ cup apple sauce or mashed banana

¼ cup vegan butter, softened (not melted)

ADD-INS (CHOOSE 1-3, OPTIONAL, SEE QUICK TIP)

½ teaspoon vanilla extract

½ teaspoon almond extract

1 teaspoon cinnamon or Pumpkin Pie Spice (page 49 or store-bought)

1–2 tablespoons lemon, lime, orange, or grapefruit zest

½ cup fresh or frozen berries

½ cup vegan chocolate chips or chopped dark chocolate

½ cup chopped apples, bananas, peaches, or other fruit

¼ cup vegan-friendly sprinkles

¼ cup chopped almonds, walnuts, pecans, pistachios, or hazelnuts

¼ cup shredded or flaked coconut

2 tablespoons poppy or sesame seeds

recipe continues

TO MAKE THE MIX

1. Add the flour, sugar, baking powder, baking soda, and salt to a large jar. Shake or stir well to combine, making sure the ingredients are evenly distributed. Store in your pantry for up to 1 year.

TO MAKE THE MUFFINS

1. Preheat your oven to 375°F. Lightly grease a six-count muffin pan or line with paper cups.

2. In a large bowl, mix together 1⅓ cups muffin mix with the plant-based milk, apple sauce or banana, and vegan butter. If you are adding any extracts, spices, or zest, add those now as well. Stir to combine, but don't overmix; lumps are totally cool. (Overmixing can result in the muffins not rising properly.) Now add any other additions, such as fruit, chocolate, nuts, coconut, or seeds.

3. Divide the muffin mix evenly among the six muffin wells and bake for 13–18 minutes, until golden and a toothpick inserted into the center comes out clean.

QUICK TIP: Feel free to play around with the flavor combos. Some of my faves are lemon and poppy seed, almond extract and vegan-friendly sprinkles (tastes like birthday cake!), blueberries and lime zest, and pumpkin pie spice and coconut.

MAKE AHEAD: You can prepare these muffins ahead of time and freeze them. Allow to cool completely, then toss in an airtight container or bag and freeze for up to 3 months. Allow muffins to thaw at room temperature.

Boxed mac & cheese was always a childhood favorite of mine. Health-food stores carry vegan versions, but honestly, they aren't that good, and they are super pricey. I much prefer the taste and price of making my own mix. Bonus points: you can also use this powder to whip up a cheese sauce to pour over veggies, tortilla chips, or fries!

MAKES | About 1 cup powder, 4 batches mac & cheese (stovetop method)

TOTAL TIME | 15 minutes

TOTAL COST FOR MIX | Under $5

COST PER BATCH OF MAC & CHEESE | Under $3

MAC & CHEESE POWDER

FOR THE MAC & CHEESE POWDER

- ¾ cup nutritional yeast
- ½ cup all-purpose flour (sub whole wheat or all-purpose gluten-free flour if preferred)
- 1 tablespoon white sugar
- 1 tablespoon paprika
- 2 teaspoons salt
- 2 teaspoons onion powder
- 1 teaspoon garlic powder
- 1 teaspoon lemon pepper
- ½ teaspoon turmeric

FOR THE MAC & CHEESE, STOVETOP METHOD (SERVES 2)

- 1 cup uncooked macaroni noodles (gluten-free if preferred)
- ¾ cup plant-based milk, such as soy or oat
- ¼ cup Mac & Cheese Powder

FOR THE MAC & CHEESE, MICROWAVE METHOD (SERVES 1)

- ½ cup uncooked macaroni noodles (gluten-free if preferred)
- ¾ cup water
- 3 tablespoons plant-based milk, such as soy or oat
- 2 tablespoons Mac & Cheese Powder

FOR THE CHEESE SAUCE (USE AS A DIP OR WITH OTHER DISHES)

- ¾ cup plant-based milk, such as soy or oat
- ¼ cup Mac & Cheese Powder

recipe continues

TO MAKE THE POWDER

1. Add the nutritional yeast, flour, sugar, paprika, salt, onion powder, garlic powder, lemon pepper, and turmeric to an airtight container. Stir or shake well to combine, making sure ingredients are evenly distributed. Store in your pantry for up to 1 year.

TO MAKE THE STOVETOP MAC & CHEESE

1. Bring a medium pot of water to a boil and cook the macaroni noodles according to package directions. Drain and rinse the pasta. Turn the heat off and return the pot to the stove.

2. Pour the plant-based milk and ¼ cup mac & cheese powder into the pot and whisk together. Turn the heat back on to medium-high and whisk until the sauce thickens, 2–5 minutes.

3. Add the cooked pasta to the pot along with the cheese sauce and stir to combine.

TO MAKE THE MICROWAVE MAC & CHEESE

1. Add the macaroni and water to a large microwave-safe mug or bowl, and mix together. Microwave on high for 2–5 minutes until the macaroni is fully cooked. Drain off any excess water.

2. Stir in the plant-based milk and 2 tablespoons mac & cheese powder and microwave 30 seconds more.

TO MAKE THE CHEESE SAUCE

1. Whisk the plant-based milk and ¼ cup mac & cheese powder together in a small pot. Turn the heat to medium-high and continue to whisk until the sauce thickens, 2–5 minutes. Alternatively, you can prepare the sauce in the microwave by whisking the sauce in a medium microwave-safe bowl. Microwave on high at 30-second increments, stopping to stir it until the sauce thickens, 2–3 minutes.

□ □

LABEL FUN

I love having jars of beautiful homemade mixes at the ready that are a fraction of the cost of store-bought blends but have all of the ease. All the directions needed for these recipes are included in this book, but I've also made labels which can be printed and pasted to your jars or stored along with your mixes for quick referencing. Visit itdoesnttastelikechicken.com/labels to download them for free!

□ □

Boxes or cans of vegetable broth can be expensive, and while boiling up a homemade broth from scratch is super affordable, it can take a bit of time and forethought. Having a jar of this powder on hand is super convenient, takes up way less shelf space, and is an affordable alternative.

MAKES | About ¼ cup powder, 12 cups veggie broth

TOTAL TIME | 10 minutes

TOTAL COST FOR MIX | Under $1

COST PER 1 CUP OF BROTH | Under $1

VEGGIE BROTH POWDER

TO MAKE THE POWDER

1. Add the dried parsley, dried thyme, onion powder, garlic powder, salt, dried basil, celery seed, pepper and turmeric to an airtight container. Stir or shake well to combine, making sure ingredients are evenly distributed. Store in your pantry for up to 3 years.

TO MAKE THE VEGGIE BROTH

1. Stir 1 teaspoon veggie broth powder into your hot water. The broth will have flecks of spices in it. If you prefer a completely smooth broth, you can allow the broth to steep for 5–10 minutes, then pour through a fine-mesh strainer.

MAKE AHEAD: Whip up this veggie broth ahead of time, let it cool, then store in an airtight jar in the fridge for 4–5 days. Shake or stir before using, as it may settle.

FOR THE VEGGIE BROTH POWDER

2 teaspoons dried parsley

2 teaspoons dried thyme leaves

2 teaspoons onion powder

2 teaspoons garlic powder

2 teaspoons salt

1 teaspoon dried basil

1 teaspoon celery seed

¼ teaspoon black pepper

½ teaspoon turmeric

FOR THE VEGGIE BROTH

1 teaspoon Veggie Broth Powder

1 cup hot water

Mushrooms are so rich and earthy, they make a great base for a vegan gravy. My grocery store sells all kinds of dried mushrooms, so I usually pick some up when they are on sale. Then I just pulse them in a coffee grinder, high-powered blender, or food processor to turn them to powder. Feel free to use whatever kind of dried mushroom you like in this recipe; each type will provide a slightly different flavor.

MAKES | About 1 cup mix, 5 batches mushroom gravy

TOTAL TIME | 15 minutes

TOTAL COST FOR MIX | Under $5

COST PER BATCH OF GRAVY | Under $1

MUSHROOM GRAVY MIX

TO MAKE THE MIX

1. To make mushroom powder, add the dried mushrooms to a coffee grinder or small food processor and blend until a powder is achieved.

2. Add the mushroom powder, flour, onion powder, garlic powder, sage, thyme, and pepper to a sealable container or jar. Stir or shake well to combine. Store in your pantry for up to 6 months

TO MAKE THE MUSHROOM GRAVY

1. In a small saucepan, whisk together the cold water, 3 tablespoons mushroom gravy mix, and 2 teaspoons soy sauce. (For a thicker gravy use 1 cup of water, for a thinner gravy use 1½.) Set over medium heat and cook, continuing to whisk often, until the gravy thickens, 2–5 minutes. Add more soy sauce to taste, if desired.

FOR THE MUSHROOM GRAVY MIX

¼ ounce dried mushrooms (2½ tablespoons powdered)

¾ cup all-purpose flour

1 tablespoon onion powder

1 tablespoon garlic powder

1 teaspoon ground sage

1 teaspoon dried thyme leaves

¼ teaspoon black pepper

FOR THE MUSHROOM GRAVY

1–1½ cups cold water

3 tablespoons Mushroom Gravy Mix

2–4 teaspoons soy sauce

MAKE AHEAD: You can make this gravy ahead of time and store it in an airtight container in the fridge for up to 3 days or in the freezer for up to 2 months. Gently reheat in a pot on the stove or in the microwave, whisking in a splash of water to thin, if needed. If frozen, thaw before reheating.

MAKES | About 8 cups mix,
4 one-layer cakes or 48 cupcakes

TOTAL TIME | 30 minutes

TOTAL COST FOR MIX | Under $3

COST PER CAKE OR BATCH OF CUPCAKES | Under $3

Whether you're celebrating a birthday or celebrating the end of the day, nothing compares to the sweet perfection of cake! With this mix you can make as many layers as you like, make cupcakes, or even make a mug cake for one. The baked result is delicious all on its own, served plain with fresh fruit, or spread with any of the Freezer Frostings (page 228).

YELLOW CAKE MIX

FOR THE YELLOW CAKE MIX

5 cups all-purpose flour

3 cups white sugar

4 teaspoons baking soda

2 teaspoons salt

1 teaspoon turmeric (for color)

FOR THE ONE-LAYER CAKE OR 12 CUPCAKES

2 cups Yellow Cake Mix

⅔ cup plant-based milk, such as soy or oat

⅓ cup light oil, such as canola or vegetable

2 tablespoons lemon juice

2 teaspoons vanilla extract

FOR THE MUG CAKE (SERVES 1)

¼ cup Yellow Cake Mix

2 tablespoons plant-based milk, such as soy or oat

1 tablespoon light oil, such as canola or vegetable

1 teaspoon vegan-friendly sprinkles (optional)

¼ teaspoon vanilla extract

TO MAKE THE MIX

1. Add the flour, sugar, baking soda, salt, and turmeric to a large jar or sealable container. Whisk well to combine, making sure ingredients are evenly distributed. Store in your pantry for up to 1 year.

TO MAKE THE ONE-LAYER CAKE OR 12 CUPCAKES

1. Preheat your oven to 350°F. Lightly grease a 9-inch round cake pan and line the bottom with parchment paper, or line a 12-count cupcake pan with liners.

2. In a large bowl, mix together 2 cups cake mix, plant-based milk, oil, lemon juice, and vanilla. Don't overmix the batter or it could result in a denser cake (lumps are totally cool).

3. For the one-layer cake: Pour the batter into the prepared pan and bake for 22–28 minutes, until lightly golden and a toothpick inserted into the center comes out clean. Allow to cool completely before removing the cake from the pan.

For the cupcakes: Divide the batter evenly among the 12 cupcake wells. Bake for 18–22 minutes, until lightly golden on top and a toothpick inserted into the center comes out clean. Let the cupcakes cool in the pan.

TO MAKE THE MUG CAKE

1. In a microwave-safe mug, mix ¼ cup cake mix, plant-based milk, oil, sprinkles, and vanilla.

2. Microwave on high for about 1 minute and 30 seconds, until the cake has risen but is still slightly damp on top. Allow to cool for 5 minutes before enjoying.

MAKE AHEAD: You can freeze baked and cooled cakes or cupcakes before they are frosted. When ready to eat, allow the cakes or cupcakes to thaw completely at room temperature (about 3 hours), and enjoy plain or spread with a thawed Freezer Frosting (page 228).

MAKES | About 8 cups mix,
4 one-layer cakes or 48 cupcakes

TOTAL TIME | 30 minutes

TOTAL COST FOR MIX | Under $7

COST PER CAKE OR BATCH OF CUPCAKES | Under $3

Anytime I see the devil's food cake mixes on the shelf, I can't help but want to rub my palms together while uttering an evil "muhaha" of a laugh. This cake may be extra-rich and chocolaty, but that ain't a bad thing in my books! The espresso powder or coffee enhances the flavor of the cocoa, making this cake taste even richer, but if you don't have it on hand or aren't a fan, you can always skip it, for a cake that's still great. This cake is wonderful enjoyed alone or with any of the Freezer Frostings (page 228).

DEVIL'S FOOD CAKE MIX

FOR THE DEVIL'S FOOD CAKE MIX

3½ cups all-purpose flour

3½ cups white sugar

1½ cups cocoa powder

4 teaspoons espresso powder (optional)

4 teaspoons baking soda

3 teaspoons baking powder

2 teaspoons salt

FOR THE ONE-LAYER CAKE OR 12 CUPCAKES

2 cups Devil's Food Cake Mix

½ cup plant-based milk, such as soy or oat

½ cup brewed hot coffee (sub hot water if preferred)

⅓ cup light oil, such as canola or vegetable

½ teaspoon vanilla extract

TO MAKE THE MIX

1. Add the flour, sugar, cocoa powder, espresso powder (if using), baking soda, baking powder, and salt to a large jar or sealable container. Whisk well to combine. Store in your pantry for up to 1 year.

TO MAKE THE ONE-LAYER CAKE OR 12 CUPCAKES

1. Preheat your oven to 350°F. Lightly grease a 9-inch round cake pan and line the bottom with parchment paper, or line a 12-count cupcake pan with liners.

2. In a large bowl, mix together 2 cups cake mix, plant-based milk, hot coffee, oil, and vanilla. Don't overmix the batter; it's okay if it has lumps.

3. For the one-layer cake: Pour and spread the batter into the prepared pan and bake for 22–26 minutes, until a toothpick inserted into the center comes out clean. Allow to cool in the pan before removing.

For the cupcakes: Divide the batter evenly among the 12 cupcake wells. Bake for 15–20 minutes, until a toothpick inserted into the center comes out clean. Allow the cupcakes to cool in the pan before removing.

TO MAKE THE MUG CAKE

1. In a microwave-safe mug, mix ¼ cup cake mix, plant-based milk, oil, coffee, chocolate chips (if using), and vanilla.

2. Microwave on high for about 1 minute and 30 seconds, until the cake has risen and looks set but is still slightly damp on top. Allow to cool for 5 minutes before enjoying. Top with ice cream, if desired.

MAKE AHEAD: You can freeze baked and cooled cakes or cupcakes before they are frosted. When ready to eat, allow the cakes or cupcakes to thaw completely at room temperature (about 3 hours), and enjoy plain or spread with a thawed Freezer Frosting (page 228).

FOR THE MUG CAKE (SERVES 1)

¼ cup Devil's Food Cake Mix

1 tablespoon plant-based milk, such as soy or oat

1 tablespoon light oil, such as canola or vegetable

1 tablespoon brewed coffee or water

1 tablespoon chocolate chips (optional)

¼ teaspoon vanilla extract

Lickety-Split Ice Cream (page 216, optional)

If you've ever looked at the ingredients of store-bought hot chocolate mixes, you likely noticed one of two things: the list of ingredients is shockingly long, with all sorts of weird ingredients you didn't know were edible, or the list is shockingly short, which might make you think, "Why in the world am I paying for this when I could make it myself?" Hot chocolate mix is easy with a capital E to make, and so much richer and tastier than the dried-out store version.

MAKES | 2 cups mix, 5 servings
TOTAL TIME | 5 minutes
TOTAL COST FOR MIX | Under $3
COST PER SERVING OF HOT CHOCOLATE | Under $1

HOT CHOCOLATE MIX

TO MAKE THE MIX

1. Add the cocoa powder, sugar, and salt to an airtight container. Stir or shake to combine, making sure ingredients are mixed well. Store in your pantry for up to 2 years.

TO MAKE THE HOT CHOCOLATE

1. Stovetop method: In a small saucepan over medium heat, mix together 3 tablespoons hot chocolate mix and the plant-based milk. Heat for about 3 minutes, until hot and everything is mixed together well. Dollop with coconut cream, if desired.

Microwave method: In a large mug, mix together 3 tablespoons hot chocolate mix and plant-based milk, making sure there is still room to allow the hot chocolate to expand without overflowing. The mix may be lumpy at first, but it will blend into the plant-based milk once warmed. Heat in the microwave for 30-second increments, stirring between each one, until the beverage is hot and mixed well. Dollop with coconut cream, if desired.

FOR THE HOT CHOCOLATE MIX

1 cup cocoa powder

1 cup white sugar

½ teaspoon salt

FOR THE HOT CHOCOLATE (SERVES 1)

3 tablespoons Hot Chocolate Mix

1 cup plant-based milk, such as soy or oat

A dollop of coconut cream (optional, for serving)

MAKE AHEAD: You can prepare hot chocolate a day in advance. Allow the prepared hot chocolate to cool completely before transferring it to the fridge. Gently reheat in a pot on the stove or in the microwave, whisking as needed.

MAKES | About ¼ cup
(each spice mix)

TOTAL TIME | 5 minutes

TOTAL COST | Under $2
(each spice mix)

You can easily buy premade spice mixes and use them for any of the recipes in this book, but if you already have a decent spice collection, it can save you a bit of coin in the long run if you mix your own. For all of these recipes, simply add the spices to a jar and shake to combine. Each recipe will stay fresh for 1–2 years.

DIY SPICE MIXES

QUICK TIPS: 1. If your store doesn't sell ground bay leaves, you can make your own from dried bay leaves. Use a spice grinder or coffee grinder to grind bay leaves into a powder. Or you can substitute the ground bay with ground sage for a different but similar seasoning. **2.** You can substitute the 1 tablespoon of celery salt with 1½ teaspoons celery seed + 1½ teaspoons salt.

ITALIAN SEASONING

1 tablespoon dried basil

1½ teaspoons dried thyme leaves

1½ teaspoons dried rosemary

1½ teaspoons dried parsley

1½ teaspoons dried oregano

1½ teaspoons onion powder

1½ teaspoons garlic powder

TACOS & MORE SEASONING

2 tablespoons chili powder

1 tablespoon ground cumin

1 tablespoon onion powder

1 tablespoon garlic powder

1 tablespoon paprika
  (use smoked paprika
  for extra yum)

1 teaspoon oregano

¼ teaspoon cayenne

GREEK SEASONING

1½ tablespoons dried oregano
1 tablespoon dried basil
1½ teaspoons dried dill
1½ teaspoons onion powder
1½ teaspoons garlic powder
1 teaspoon salt
½ teaspoon black pepper

PUMPKIN PIE SPICE

2 tablespoons cinnamon
1½ teaspoons ground ginger
1½ teaspoons ground nutmeg
1½ teaspoons ground allspice
¾ teaspoon ground cloves

NEW BAY SEASONING

1 tablespoon ground bay leaves (see Quick Tip)
1 tablespoon celery salt (see Quick Tip)
2 teaspoons paprika
1 teaspoon black pepper
1 teaspoon dry mustard
¼ teaspoon cayenne
⅛ teaspoon ground nutmeg
⅛ teaspoon cinnamon
⅛ teaspoon ground cloves

CAJUN SEASONING

1 tablespoon smoked paprika
2 teaspoons garlic powder
1½ teaspoons salt
1½ teaspoons black pepper
1 teaspoon onion powder
1 teaspoon dried oregano
1 teaspoon dried thyme leaves
1 teaspoon cayenne (optional)

SERVES | 1 (per smoothie kit)

TOTAL TIME | 5 minutes per smoothie

COST PER SMOOTHIE | $1–$5 (depending on your choices)

Smoothies are a great way to use leftovers and food that is about to go off. Overripe fruit is sweeter and will taste even better in a smoothie. But you can go beyond fruit. I chop and freeze avocado that's starting to go brown, as well as spinach and chopped kale that I can't get through. Spend 20–30 minutes assembling multiple smoothie kits ahead of time, and a delicious smoothie will just be a grab and blend away!

GRAB ⁝ BLEND SMOOTHIE KITS

FRESH OR FROZEN FRUIT (1 CUP, CHOOSE 1 OR A COMBO)

Blueberries	Cherries	Kiwi
Strawberries	Peaches	Apple
Mixed berries	Pineapple	Banana

ADD SOME CREAMINESS (CHOOSE 1)

1 fresh or frozen banana	½ cup chopped fresh or frozen avocados	¼ cup whole rolled or quick oats (gluten-free if preferred)
½ cup fresh or frozen mangoes	½ cup silken tofu	

AMP IT UP (CHOOSE 1–3, OPTIONAL)

1 handful fresh or frozen spinach	1 tablespoon cocoa powder	¼ teaspoon cinnamon
1 handful fresh or frozen kale leaves or stems	½ cup coffee ice cubes	¼ teaspoon Pumpkin Pie Spice (page 49 or store-bought)
1 tablespoon peanut butter or other nut butter	2 teaspoons instant espresso powder	2–4 dates (for sweetness)
	1 small handful fresh mint leaves	¼ cup raisins (for sweetness)

LIQUID (1–2 CUPS, CHOOSE 1)

Plant-based milk,
  such as soy
  or oat

Water
Fruit juice
Cooled coffee

Cooled herbal tea
Coconut water

1. For each smoothie kit, add 1 cup fruit of choice (or combination of fruits), one creamy ingredient, and one to three amp-it-up ingredients, if desired, to a small bag or container, and freeze (I use reusable freezer bags). I like to make several smoothie kits at a time so I always have one ready to go.

2. When ready to blend, simply dump one of the frozen smoothie kits into a blender and add 1 cup liquid of choice, adding more liquid as needed to reach the desired consistency.

SERVES | 4

TOTAL TIME | 20 minutes

TOTAL COST | Under $7

When the first thing you take a bite of in the morning is a savory sandwich, stacked with layers of thin, crisp, eggy-flavored tofu, you know it's gonna be a good day! Don't be fooled by the simplicity of these breakfast sandwiches. They are packed full of flavor. That said, if you want to play around with additional veg toppings, go for it!

20-MINUTE BREAKFAST SANDWICHES

FOR THE TOFU SEASONING

¼ cup Tofu Scramble
    Seasoning (page 27,
    see Quick Tip)

2 tablespoons cornstarch

FOR THE SANDWICHES

1 block (12 ounces) extra-firm
    or firm tofu, drained and
    thinly sliced into about
    12 slices

Oil or vegan butter, for frying

4 English muffins or bagels,
    halved and toasted
    (gluten-free if preferred)

Optional toppings: sliced
    tomatoes, lettuce leaves,
    sliced onions, sliced
    avocados, or any toppings
    you desire!

¼ cup ketchup

1. In a wide bowl, mix together the tofu scramble seasoning and cornstarch.

2. Take a slice of the tofu and dip both sides into the spice mixture. The tofu has enough moisture in it that the seasoning should stick well. Repeat with the remaining slices.

3. Heat the oil or butter in a skillet or frying pan, then fry the slices in a single layer, 1–3 minutes on each side, until they just begin to brown. Repeat with all slices, working in batches if needed.

4. To assemble the sandwiches, top one half of each English muffin or bagel with three fried slices of tofu, followed by any toppings and 1 tablespoon ketchup. Top with the remaining half of the bread and enjoy the sandwiches hot.

The perfect recipe for a day when you have nothing in your cupboard except a couple of potatoes. These potato pancakes hold together beautifully without any kind of egg or egg replacement needed! The outside gets golden and crispy, and the inside stays tender. I love these for a savory breakfast with ketchup and Sriracha, but feel free to enjoy them any time of day.

MAKES | About 10 pancakes, 4 servings

TOTAL TIME | 25 minutes

TOTAL COST | Under $5

MORNING RUSH POTATO PANCAKES

1. Add the potatoes, yellow onions, flour, green onions, garlic, salt, pepper, and baking powder to a large bowl and mix well.

2. Add 1 tablespoon of oil to a large skillet or frying pan and set over medium-high heat. When the oil is hot, take a handful of the potato mixture and form into a loose patty (see Quick Tip). The mixture will be very wet and soft. Carefully drop the patty directly into the hot pan. Fry for 2–3 minutes, until the bottom is golden brown, then flip and fry on the other side, until golden brown. Drain the pancake on paper towel. Repeat with the remaining potato mixture, adding more oil to the pan as needed.

3 medium Yukon gold or russet potatoes, scrubbed clean (no need to peel) and grated

½ yellow onion, grated

½ cup all-purpose flour (gluten-free if preferred)

2 green onions, chopped

2 cloves garlic, minced or pressed

1 teaspoon salt

¼ teaspoon black pepper

¼ teaspoon baking powder

Light oil, such as canola or vegetable, for frying

QUICK TIP: For extra-crispy potato pancakes, make the patties very thin.

MAKE AHEAD: The potato pancakes can be cooked, cooled, and then stored in the fridge for up to 2 days. To warm, preheat your oven to 375°F and bake for 10–15 minutes until heated through.

SERVES | 1
TOTAL TIME | 10 minutes
TOTAL COST | $1–$3
(depending on your choices)

Do not underestimate the power of toast! If you think toast is boring, then let me reintroduce you. It can be so much more than just a pat of vegan butter. Not only is it super quick and easy, but it can be topped with endless combinations. Savory, sweet, spicy, smooth, crunchy—it never gets dull!

TOAST IS THE MOST!

BREAD (CHOOSE 1, GLUTEN-FREE IF PREFERRED)

1 slice bread

1 piece baguette

1 bagel

1 English muffin

SPREAD (CHOOSE 1)

½ avocado, mashed

2 tablespoons peanut butter

2 tablespoons other nut or seed butter

2 tablespoons vegan cream cheese

2 tablespoons classic hummus

2 tablespoons flavored hummus

2 tablespoons Hummamole (page 84)

¼ cup beans, mashed

¼ cup lentils

2 tablespoons canned refried beans (check to make sure they're vegan)

TOPPINGS (CHOOSE 1–2)

½ banana, sliced

½ apple, sliced

½ cup sliced strawberries

¼ tomato, sliced

½ pear, sliced

¼ cup blueberries

½ cup raspberries

1 small handful arugula

1 lettuce leaf

2–3 radishes, sliced

¼ cup sliced cucumbers

¼ cup raisins

2 tablespoons jam or jelly

1 wedge cantaloupe, sliced

¼ cup pineapple slices or pieces

FLAVOR BOOSTERS (CHOOSE 1-3, OPTIONAL)

Fresh basil leaves

Fresh mint leaves

Fresh cilantro leaves

1 tablespoon chopped walnuts

1 tablespoon sliced almonds

2 teaspoons balsamic vinegar or glaze

1 tablespoon maple syrup

1 tablespoon agave

1 tablespoon vegan barbecue sauce

1 tablespoon shredded coconut

1 tablespoon sesame seeds

1 tablespoon poppy seeds

Lime, lemon, or orange zest

1 tablespoon nutritional yeast

⅛ red onion, thinly sliced

1 tablespoon sliced green onions or chives

1 tablespoon sliced olives

2 teaspoons capers

¼–½ teaspoon Spice Mix of choice (page 48)

¼–½ teaspoon cinnamon

Salt and black pepper

---

1. Toast your bread of choice.

2. Add a spread, one to two toppings, and any desired flavor boosters. Enjoy!

recipe continues

PB:S

AVOCADO ARUGULA

PEAR WALNUT

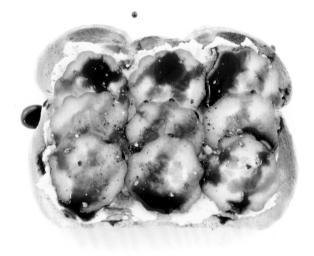

HUMMUS CUCUMBER

BBQ LENTIL

BANANA RAISIN

RADISH CILANTRO

CREAM CHEESE CANTALOUPE

LEMON RASPBERRY

◇ ◇

SOME OF MY FAVORITE COMBOS

Avocado Arugula: Avocado, arugula, red onion, and a sprinkle of Cajun spice mix.

Pear Walnut: Vegan cream cheese, slices of pear, walnuts, maple syrup, and cinnamon.

Hummus Cucumber: Hummus, cucumber, balsamic glaze, and black pepper.

BBQ Lentil: Lentils mixed with barbecue sauce, tomato slices, nutritional yeast, salt, and pepper.

Banana Raisin: Peanut butter, banana, raisins, and shredded coconut.

Radish Cilantro: Hummamole (page 84), radish slices, cilantro, salt, and pepper.

Cream Cheese Cantaloupe: Vegan cream cheese, cantaloupe, sliced almonds, and agave.

Lemon Raspberry: Vegan cream cheese, raspberries, lemon zest, and poppy seeds.

PB&S: Peanut butter, strawberry slices, and lime zest.

◇ ◇

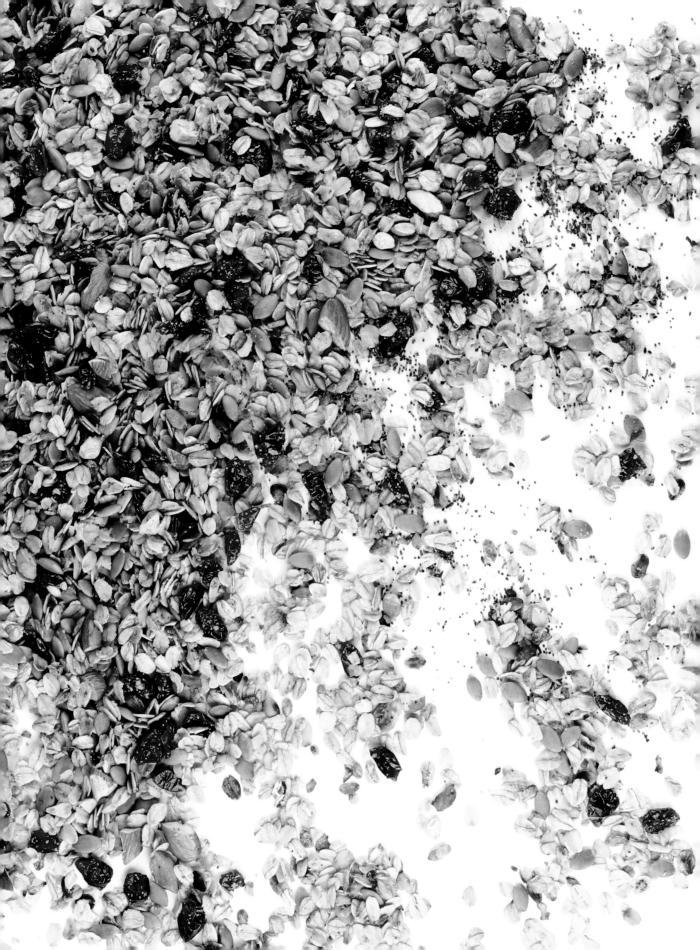

Granola can be crazy-expensive at the store, but is actually really affordable to make at home. This stovetop method is so quick and easy to prepare, I love whipping up a fresh batch while I wait for the water to boil for my coffee. This is the perfect recipe to make ahead of time and store in an airtight jar. Serve this with some vegan yogurt or plant-based milk with fresh fruit, or snack on it plain. I love this granola served still warm from the skillet.

QUICK STOVETOP GRANOLA

1. In a large skillet over medium-high heat, melt the vegan butter. Once melted, add the oats, seeds and/or nuts, syrup, cinnamon, and salt. Stir the mixture as it toasts, until the oats turn golden and everything is evenly coated, about 5 minutes.

2. Remove from heat and add the dried fruit. Let cool before storing—it'll crisp up as it cools.

MAKE AHEAD: Store in an airtight container in your pantry for up to 6 months.

MAKES | About 4 cups granola, 8 servings

TOTAL TIME | 10 minutes

TOTAL COST | $3–$7 (depending on your choices)

2 tablespoons vegan butter or coconut oil

2 cups whole rolled oats (gluten-free if preferred)

½ cup sunflower seeds, pepitas, raw peanuts, flax seeds, sesame seeds, shredded coconut, poppy seeds, chopped almonds, or any other nut or seed you like, or a combination.

¼ cup corn syrup, agave, or maple syrup

½ teaspoon cinnamon or Pumpkin Pie Spice (page 49 or store-bought, optional)

¼ teaspoon salt

½ cup raisins, dried cranberries, or other dried fruit

SERVES | 4
TOTAL TIME | 20 minutes
TOTAL COST | Under $10

For those who love a savory breakfast, this hash is for you! The potatoes and black beans are simmered in spicy salsa—my hack for adding a ton of flavor and tomatoey goodness in one go. Top with a dollop of quick guacamole and cilantro for a hearty, spicy, zesty morning meal. Have leftovers? Pack them up for lunch!

HASH IN A DASH

FOR THE HASH

1 tablespoon light oil, such as canola or vegetable

1 russet potato, scrubbed clean (no need to peel) and chopped into ½-inch cubes (see Quick Tip)

1 yellow onion, chopped

½ cup spicy salsa (sub mild or medium if preferred)

¼–½ cup water

1 can (19 ounces) black beans, drained and rinsed (about 2 cups)

¼–1 teaspoon salt

FOR THE TOPPINGS

2 avocados, peeled and pitted

2 tablespoons lime juice (about 1 lime)

¼ teaspoon salt

1 handful fresh cilantro, roughly chopped, for garnish

1. In a large lidded skillet or non-stick frying pan, heat the oil over medium-high heat. When hot, add the potatoes and onions and sauté for about 5 minutes, until they begin to brown. The potatoes may stick to the pan a bit, so just let them cook, and as they brown they should easily release from the pan with a gentle push. Add the salsa and ¼ cup water, then cover. Continue to cook for about 5 minutes, until the potatoes are fork-tender. You may need to add up to ¼ cup more water if the potatoes start to dry out too much.

2. Add the beans and heat through, another 3–5 minutes. Add salt to taste (this will vary depending on the salsa used). Remove from the heat.

3. In a small bowl, mash the avocados with the lime juice and salt.

4. Serve the hash with a large dollop of the mashed avocados and garnish with cilantro.

QUICK TIP: For a variation, try subbing the russet potato with sweet potato.

MAKE AHEAD: The hash can be made ahead of time, cooled, and then stored in the fridge in an airtight container for up to 2 days. Gently reheat in a skillet or in the microwave and then add the fresh toppings.

MAKES | 12–14 cookies
TOTAL TIME | 26 minutes
TOTAL COST | Under $5

Chewy, lightly sweet, and packed full of nutritious goodies, these are cookies that you can eat for breakfast! It's super easy to whip up a large batch, and then you'll have cookies that will last you the whole week. They keep fresh for several days, but also freeze beautifully, so feel free to stock that freezer. Grab a cookie or two and go!

OATMEAL BREAKFAST COOKIES

¾ cup mashed banana (2–3 bananas)

½ cup crunchy or smooth peanut butter or other nut or seed butter

¼ cup warm water

¼ cup all-purpose flour (gluten-free if preferred)

¼ cup brown sugar

2 tablespoons ground chia seeds or ground flax seeds

1 teaspoon cinnamon

¼ teaspoon salt

2½ cups quick oats (gluten-free if preferred)

½ cup add-in of choice (raisins, chopped nuts, chopped dried fruit, or vegan chocolate chips)

1. Preheat your oven to 350°F. Lightly grease a baking sheet or line with parchment paper.

2. In a large bowl, mix together the mashed bananas, peanut butter, and warm water. Add the flour, sugar, ground chia, cinnamon, and salt, and combine. Add the oats and add-in of choice and finish mixing. The dough will be quite thick, so I find it's helpful to get in there with your hands.

3. The cookies don't change shape when baked, so take ¼-cup portions of cookie dough and roll them into balls, then flatten with your hand. Place them on the baking sheet a couple of inches apart. Bake 12–16 minutes, until set and lightly browned on the bottom. Allow cookies to cool before enjoying.

MAKE AHEAD: Once cool, store cookies in an airtight container in the fridge for up to 1 week or in the freezer for up to 3 months. They thaw at room temperature in about 30 minutes, but I often enjoy them straight from the freezer. Breakfast to go!

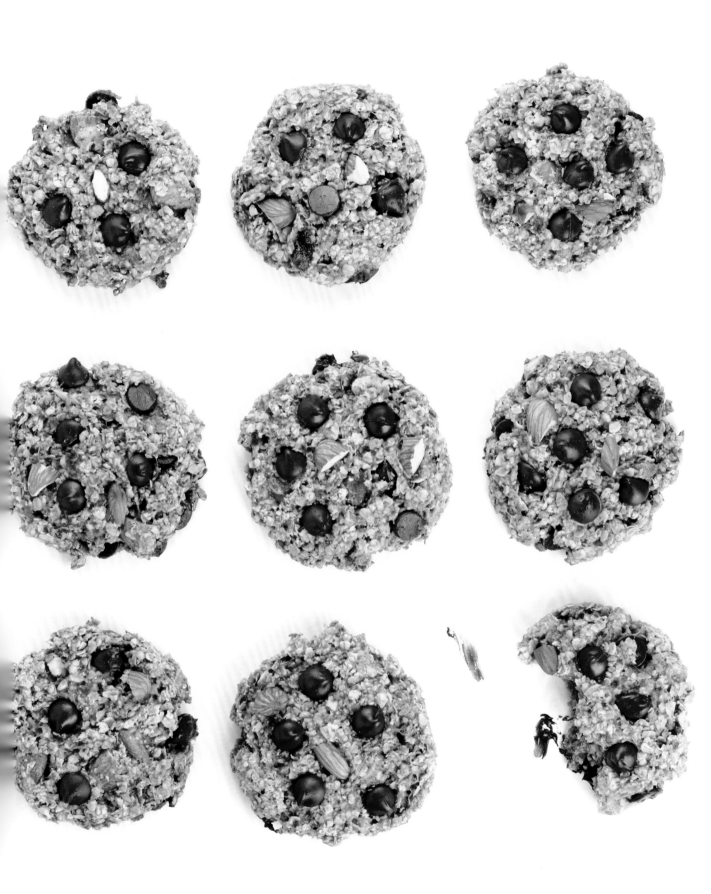

French toast doesn't have to be a luxury saved for leisurely mornings, and my individualized version takes only 3 minutes to make. This recipe works best with sturdier bread, so it's a fantastic way to use up bread ends or bread that has gone a bit stale. If you want to make more than one serving, line up the mugs and ingredients and let everyone assemble and top their own.

SERVES | 1

TOTAL TIME | 3 minutes

TOTAL COST | Under $1
(not including toppings)

FRENCH TOAST IN A MUG

1. Add the banana to a microwave-safe mug and mash with a fork. Add the plant-based milk, maple syrup, butter, cinnamon, and vanilla and mix. It's OK if it's lumpy. Add the bread pieces and toss to coat.

2. Microwave for about 60 seconds, until the mixture is hot and the bread has absorbed the liquid. Enjoy hot with your favorite toppings.

¼ medium banana

3 tablespoons plant-based milk, such as soy or oat

1 teaspoon maple syrup

1 teaspoon vegan butter (optional for flavor)

¼ teaspoon cinnamon

¼ teaspoon vanilla extract

1 slice bread, torn into pieces (about 1 cup, gluten-free if preferred)

Optional toppings: sliced fruit, berries, nuts, more maple syrup, chocolate chips, powdered sugar, or a drizzle of nut butter

At my grocery store, you can buy a 2-pound bag of instant oats for less than a box of instant oatmeal packets that contains only a fraction of the oats. If that isn't a markup, then I don't know what is! Not only are those oatmeal packets way overpriced, they usually aren't vegan or very tasty. Making your own is so easy, and you can customize them to your own preference. Make a bunch at once so you always have an easy breakfast or snack ready to go for lazy mornings or an at-the-office pick-me-up.

SERVES | 1 (per oatmeal packet)
TOTAL TIME | 10 minutes
COST PER PACKET | Under $1

DIY INSTANT OATMEAL PACKETS

1. For each oatmeal packet, add the oats, sugar (as much or as little as you like, depending on sweetness preference), and salt to a small resealable bag or airtight container. Add your preferred add-ins. Store the sealed packets in your cupboard for up to 1 year.

2. Kettle method: When ready to enjoy, pour the packet into a bowl or mug and add ¾–1 cup boiling water (depending on how liquidy you like your oatmeal), stir, and let sit for 5 minutes, until oats absorb most of the liquid. Stir and enjoy!

Microwave method: Pour the packet into a bowl or mug and add ¾–1 cup cold water or plant-based milk and microwave for 1–2 minutes, until most of the liquid is absorbed. Stir and enjoy!

QUICK TIP: You can make your own quick oats from whole rolled oats, saving you the need to buy many different types. Just pulse the whole rolled oats in the food processor until they are broken up into pieces about half the size. Presto! Instant oats.

FOR EVERY OATMEAL PACKET

⅓ cup quick oats (gluten-free if preferred, see Quick Tip)

1–3 teaspoons brown sugar or white sugar (optional)

Pinch of salt

ADD-INS (CHOOSE 1–4)

2 tablespoons shredded coconut

2 tablespoons dried fruit (chopped if pieces are large), such as cranberries, raisins, apricots, apples, prunes, dates, or figs

2 tablespoons freeze-dried fruit

1 tablespoon chopped nuts, such as peanuts, almonds, or walnuts

½ tablespoon seeds, such as flax, chia, sesame, or poppy

¼ teaspoon cinnamon

¼ teaspoon Pumpkin Pie Spice (page 49 or store-bought)

LIQUID (¾–1 CUP, CHOOSE 1)

Boiling water (for kettle method)

Cold water or plant-based milk, such as soy or oat (for microwave method)

Microwave popcorn usually isn't vegan-friendly, and it's always quite pricey. Buying popcorn kernels is so much more affordable, the popcorn is just as easy to make, and you can flavor it any way you please. Use this recipe to make classic buttery popcorn by drizzling melted vegan butter on top. You can also keep the popcorn plain or use any of the recipes in this section (pages 76–80) to kick it up a notch.

SERVES | 2

TOTAL TIME | 4 minutes

TOTAL COST | Under $1 (not including toppings) or under $3 (with toppings)

DIY MICROWAVE POPCORN

1. Add the popcorn kernels to the paper bag and fold the top over twice to seal in. Microwave on high for 2–3 minutes until 2 seconds pass between kernels popping.

2. Remove from the microwave, but be careful opening the bag, as there will be steam. Pour into a large bowl and season with toppings, if desired.

⅓ cup popcorn kernels

1 large brown paper bag

TOPPINGS (OPTIONAL)

2–4 tablespoons melted vegan butter

1–2 tablespoons nutritional yeast (for a cheesy flavor)

½ teaspoon salt

SERVES | 2
TOTAL TIME | 10 minutes
TOTAL COST | Under $3

Warning: this popcorn is so good that you may be completely distracted while watching your movie and need to rewind once the bowl is empty. This creamy, sweet, and salty popcorn is intended for sharing, so don't be surprised when someone else's hand is always in the way when you reach for your share.

PEANUT BUTTER POPCORN

⅓ cup popcorn kernels

2 tablespoons vegan butter

2 tablespoons white sugar

2 tablespoons natural peanut butter (sub other nut or seed butter if preferred)

¼ teaspoon salt

1. Pop the popcorn using the DIY Microwave Popcorn method (page 75, step 1) or with an air popper.

2. In the meantime, add the vegan butter, sugar, peanut butter, and salt to a small pot. Set over medium heat and stir together until the sugar is dissolved, about 3 minutes. Alternatively, add the ingredients to a microwave-safe bowl and cook in 20-second increments, stopping to stir until the sugar is dissolved.

3. Drizzle the peanut butter sauce over the popped popcorn while shaking the bowl. Stir to mix if needed. Let the popcorn cool for a few minutes before enjoying, as it will be hot!

If you're a fan of cinnamon, you will go crazy for this popcorn! Every crispy bite is sweet and bursting with cinnamon zing. It's the comfort of the classic cinnamon bun, but without the bakery price, bakery, or time in the kitchen.

SERVES | 2
TOTAL TIME | 7 minutes
TOTAL COST | Under $1

CINNAMON BUN POPCORN

1. Pop the popcorn using the DIY Microwave Popcorn method (page 75, step 1) or with an air popper.

2. In a small saucepan or microwave-safe bowl, mix together the vegan butter, brown sugar, cinnamon, and salt. Heat, stirring often, until the sugar is dissolved, about 2 minutes on the stove or 50 seconds in the microwave. Drizzle the cinnamon mixture over the popcorn, shaking or stirring to evenly coat the popcorn. Be careful, as it may be hot!

⅓ cup popcorn kernels
2 tablespoons vegan butter
2 tablespoons brown sugar
1 teaspoon cinnamon
¼ teaspoon salt

**SERVES | ** 2
**TOTAL TIME | ** 13 minutes
**TOTAL COST | ** Under $1

I enjoy a big bowl of popcorn most nights of the week, and this pizza popcorn reminds me of pizza buns I would get from the bakery as a kid. The tomato sauce flavor comes from using the leftover oil in a jar of sun-dried tomatoes (it's doubly satisfying finding creative uses for things you would otherwise throw out). Seasoned with classic pizza spices and a little nutritional yeast for that cheesy taste, it's like pizza in bite-size pieces!

PIZZA POPCORN

⅓ cup popcorn kernels

2 tablespoons nutritional yeast

½ teaspoon dried basil

¼ teaspoon onion powder

¼ teaspoon garlic powder

¼ teaspoon salt

2 tablespoons oil from jar of sun-dried tomatoes

1. Pop the popcorn in a microwave using the DIY Microwave Popcorn method (page 75, step 1) or with an air popper.

2. In a small bowl, mix together the nutritional yeast, dried basil, onion powder, garlic powder, and salt. Use a fork to smash the powder and break up the nutritional yeast flakes into a fine powder. This will help the seasoning better adhere to the popcorn.

3. Drizzle the popped popcorn with the sun-dried tomato oil, then sprinkle the powder mixture overtop and shake or toss well to coat evenly.

This popcorn topping is lightly cheesy with lots of cooling herb flavors, and tastes similar to those store-bought chips, but is much tastier, much cheaper, and much vegan-er. This recipe makes enough for one bowl of popcorn, but feel free to make a double, triple, or quadruple batch of the seasoning to have on hand, stored in a shaker so you will have it when cool ranch cravings strike (which, you'll soon discover, will be often)!

SERVES | 2
TOTAL TIME | 7 minutes
TOTAL COST | Under $3

COOL RANCH POPCORN

1. Pop the popcorn in a microwave using the DIY Microwave Popcorn method (page 75, step 1) or with an air popper.

2. In a small bowl or shaker, mix together the nutritional yeast, onion powder, parsley, chives, dill, garlic powder, and salt. Use a fork to smash up the nutritional yeast flakes into a fine powder so it sticks better to the popcorn.

3. Drizzle the popcorn with melted butter and season with the spice mix to taste.

⅓ cup popcorn kernels

2 tablespoons nutritional yeast

1 teaspoon onion powder

1 teaspoon dried parsley

1 teaspoon dried chives

½ teaspoon dried dill

½ teaspoon garlic powder

½ teaspoon salt

2–4 tablespoons melted vegan butter (depending on how buttery you like your popcorn)

MAKE AHEAD: You can make the cool ranch spice mix ahead of time, but the popcorn should be popped fresh. Store the seasoning in a jar in your pantry for up to 2 years.

SERVES | 2
TOTAL TIME | 7 minutes
TOTAL COST | Under $3

This slightly sweet, smoky, salty popcorn goodness scratches that salty junk food craving. You'll probably find yourself licking your fingers and sweeping up every last sprinkle of seasoning from the bottom of the bowl. Make extra of this seasoning and store it in a jar so you can sprinkle away as desired.

CHEESY BBQ POPCORN

⅓ cup popcorn kernels

2 tablespoons nutritional yeast

¾ teaspoon salt

½ teaspoon smoked paprika

½ teaspoon chili powder

½ teaspoon onion powder

½ teaspoon garlic powder

½ teaspoon white sugar

2–4 tablespoons melted vegan butter (depending on how buttery you like your popcorn)

1. Pop the popcorn in the microwave using the DIY Microwave Popcorn method (page 75, step 1) or with an air popper.

2. Add the nutritional yeast, salt, paprika, chili powder, onion powder, garlic powder, and sugar to a small bowl or shaker. Use a fork to smash the nutritional yeast flakes into a fine powder so that it better adheres to the popcorn.

3. Drizzle the popcorn with the melted butter and toss well to evenly coat. Sprinkle all of the spice mix overtop, and again toss well to evenly coat.

QUICK TIP: If you want cheesy BBQ, cool ranch (page 79), pizza (page 78), or cinnamon bun (page 77) flavored chips, pick up a bag of plain tortilla chips, lay them out in a single layer, spritz with a bit of lime juice or melted vegan butter, and sprinkle them with your preferred seasoning.

MAKE AHEAD: The spice mixture can be prepared ahead of time and stored in an airtight container in the pantry for up to 1 year, but the popcorn should be popped fresh.

Usually pinwheels are spread with cream cheese. Sure, you can use vegan cream cheese, but I like to use mashed white beans instead. It's healthier, cheaper, and super tasty. The cranberries make these little bites slightly sweet, which I love, but if you want a more savory version, feel free to sub the cranberries and parsley with equal amounts of chopped sun-dried tomatoes and fresh basil.

SERVES | 2–4
TOTAL TIME | 10 minutes
TOTAL COST | Under $5

WHITE BEAN PINWHEELS

1. Add the beans to a medium bowl and use a potato masher or fork to smash them until they reach a spreadable consistency. (It's OK if some bean pieces are still left.) Add the cranberries, parsley, mayonnaise, mustard, seasoning, and salt and mix together.

2. Lay a tortilla flat on your work surface and spread one-quarter of the bean mixture all over the tortilla. Roll the tortilla up tightly. Use a sharp knife to slice the roll into 2-inch-wide rounds. Repeat with the remaining tortillas. Serve freshly made.

1 can (19 ounces) white kidney beans, drained and rinsed (about 2 cups)

½ cup dried cranberries

½ cup chopped fresh parsley

3 tablespoons vegan mayonnaise

1 tablespoon Dijon mustard

1 teaspoon Italian Seasoning (page 48 or store-bought)

½ teaspoon salt

4 large flour tortillas (gluten-free if preferred)

MAKES | About 4 cups

TOTAL TIME | 15 minutes

TOTAL COST | Under $7
(dip only)

What do you get when you combine guacamole and hummus? The perfect party pleaser, that's what. Avocado makes this hummus so creamy and light, you won't ever want to have avocado-free hummus again!

HUMMAMOLE

1 can (19 ounces) chickpeas, drained and rinsed (about 2 cups)

2 avocados, peeled and pitted

¼ cup lime juice (about 2 limes)

3 tablespoons olive oil

2 tablespoons tahini

2 cloves garlic, peeled

¾ teaspoon salt

¼ teaspoon black pepper

1 small handful fresh cilantro, roughly chopped, for garnish (optional)

½ teaspoon crushed red pepper flakes, for garnish (optional)

Tortilla chips, crackers, pita triangles, or veggies, for serving (gluten-free if preferred)

1. Add the chickpeas, avocados, lime juice, oil, tahini, garlic, salt, and pepper to a food processor and blend until completely smooth and creamy, stopping to scrape the sides as needed.

2. Scoop the dip into a bowl and garnish with cilantro and red pepper flakes, if desired. Serve with your favorite dipper—tortilla chips, crackers, pita triangles, and veggies all work well.

MAKE AHEAD: The lime in this recipe not only adds zing, but also keeps the avocado fresh, so you can store this dip in an airtight container in the fridge for up to 5 days.

This creamy dip is bursting with the gorgeous flavor of sweet potato and a zing of lime. So easy to whip up and so scrumptious, this dip has become a staple in our house! I love serving this with toasted pita triangles, but if you're lucky enough to have leftovers, it also makes a great toast spread.

MAKES | About 3 cups
TOTAL TIME | 15 minutes
TOTAL COST | Under $5 (dip only)

SWEET POTATO DIP

1. Prick the sweet potato all over with a fork (to allow steam to release). Place on a microwave-safe plate and microwave on high for about 8 minutes, until the potato is soft all the way through when pierced with a knife.

2. Cut the sweet potato in half (allowing the potato to cool first if needed) and scoop the flesh out, discarding the skin. Add the sweet potato flesh, beans, 3 tablespoons coconut milk, lime juice, garlic, salt, and pepper to a food processor or blender and combine, stopping to scrape the sides as needed. If your dip is too thick, add up to 3 tablespoons more coconut milk as needed to reach your preferred dip consistency. Garnish with lime zest and olive oil, if desired, and serve with pita triangles, chips, or veggies.

1 medium sweet potato (about 13 ounces)

1 can (19 ounces) white beans, such as kidney or navy, drained and rinsed (about 2 cups)

3–6 tablespoons full-fat coconut milk

3 tablespoons lime juice (about 1½ limes)

1 clove garlic

1 teaspoon salt

½ teaspoon black pepper

Lime zest and olive oil, for garnish (optional)

Pita triangles, tortilla chips, or veggies, for serving (gluten-free if preferred)

QUICK TIP: I love the flavor coconut milk adds, but you can sub with another plant-based milk if you prefer.

MAKE AHEAD: Store this dip in an airtight container in the fridge for up to 5 days.

MAKES | About 2 cups
TOTAL TIME | 5 minutes
TOTAL COST | $1–$10
(depending on your choices)

When I get the munchies, I get them BAD! Making trail mix is not only the ultimate munchie satisfier, but also a great way to use up those last bits of cereal in the box or the remaining pretzels after a party. Peanuts are one of the most affordable nuts and, in my opinion, are one of the most delicious too, so I usually make them the base of my trail mix. Then, if the mood strikes, I'll add other nuts to amp it up a little.

MIX 'N' MATCH TRAIL MIX

NUTS & SEEDS (¾ CUP, ANY NUT OR SEED OR A COMBO)

Peanuts	Cashews	Sunflower seeds
Almonds	Hazelnuts	Pepitas (pumpkin seeds)
Walnuts	Pecans	Other nuts or seeds

CHEWY BITES (½ CUP, CHOOSE 1 OR A COMBO)

Raisins	Dried blueberries	Prunes, chopped
Dried cranberries	Dates, chopped	Other dried fruit
Dried figs, chopped		

CRISPY BITES (½ CUP, CHOOSE 1 OR A COMBO)

Mini pretzels

Popcorn (pages 75–80)

Cereal

Potato chips

Banana chips

Broken or small crackers

Sesame sticks

EXTRA PUNCH (¼ CUP, CHOOSE 1, OPTIONAL)

Vegan chocolate chips

Crystalized ginger

Wasabi peas

Shredded coconut

Broken or small cookies

Seaweed rice crackers

---

1. To a medium bowl or sealable container, add ¾ cup nuts and/or seeds, ½ cup chewy bites, ½ cup crispy bites, and an extra punch ingredient, if desired. Mix together and enjoy.

ᴅ ᴅ

QUICK TIPS: 1. I love buying roasted and salted nuts for an extra flavor punch. **2.** If your grocery store carries it, freeze-dried fruit is another fun add-in!

MAKE AHEAD: Store in an airtight container in your pantry for up to 1 month.

ᴅ ᴅ

MAKES | About 1½ cups

TOTAL TIME | 5 minutes
(plus overnight to chill the
coconut milk)

TOTAL COST | Under $5
(not including fruit) or under
$10 (with fruit)

1 can (13.5 ounces) coconut
  cream or full-fat coconut
  milk, refrigerated overnight
  (about 1¾ cups, see
  Quick Tip)

1–2 tablespoons maple syrup,
  agave, or corn syrup

½ teaspoon vanilla extract

Plant-based milk (optional)

Lime zest (optional)

Fruit, for serving

This cool, creamy coconut dip pairs perfectly with fresh fruit—
I love it with strawberries and watermelon in the summer, and
apples and banana slices in the winter. It also works gorgeously
as a dessert topping. Try dolloping it on waffles (page 28) or
Fast Fried Cinnamon Sugar Bananas (page 199), or enjoy it
with cookies!

COOL COCONUT FRUIT DIP

1. Into a small bowl, scoop the chilled coconut cream out of the
can, leaving behind any coconut water.

2. Add 1 tablespoon syrup of choice and vanilla and stir to combine.
Add more syrup if desired. If the coconut cream is too thick, you
can add a splash of the leftover coconut water or a splash of
plant-based milk to thin as needed. Garnish with lime zest, if
desired. Serve with your favorite fruit and dip away.

QUICK TIPS: 1. If you don't have access to coconut cream, try to find
an extra-rich coconut milk so you get the most cream for your buck.
You can compare nutrition information on the back of the cans to
find the one highest in fat. My favorite brand has 13 grams of fat in
a ⅓-cup serving. **2.** Save the leftover coconut water and toss it in
a smoothie. It should stay fresh in the fridge for 1–2 days. **3.** For a
strawberry-flavored fruit dip, sub the syrup with strawberry jam.

MAKE AHEAD: You can make this fruit dip ahead of time and store
in an airtight container in the fridge until ready to serve. It will keep
fresh for up to 1 week.

Crispy, crunchy, cheesy, and salty, these little munchies are perfect for on-the-go. Don't be intimidated making your own crackers—it's actually so, so easy. You can make these ahead of time and store them in an airtight container at room temperature for about a week . . . but don't be surprised when they don't last even an hour.

MAKES | About 100 crackers
TOTAL TIME | 25 minutes
TOTAL COST | Under $3

CHEESY CRACKER SNACKERS

1. Preheat your oven to 350°F. Line a large baking sheet with parchment paper.

2. Add the flour, nutritional yeast, salt, onion powder, garlic powder, baking powder, and turmeric to a food processor and pulse to combine. Add the vegan butter and pulse again until you reach a crumbly texture. Add 3 tablespoons water and pulse until mixed in. Add 1 tablespoon more water as needed until the mixture looks crumbly and easily holds together when pinched.

3. Dump the contents of the food processor out onto a clean work surface and use your hands to gather the mixture together into a tight dough ball. Set aside.

4. Lay a sheet of parchment paper on your work surface or lightly sprinkle the work surface with flour. Place the dough on top of the prepared surface and roll out to about ⅛-inch thickness. Use a knife or pizza cutter to cut the dough into a grid pattern, making 1-inch square crackers.

5. Separate the crackers and spread them out in a single layer on the prepared baking sheet. Bake for 12–15 minutes, until the edges on some crackers just start to brown. Let cool for 5 minutes before enjoying.

1 cup all-purpose flour
¼ cup nutritional yeast
½ teaspoon salt
½ teaspoon onion powder
½ teaspoon garlic powder
½ teaspoon baking powder
¼ teaspoon turmeric
¼ cup cold vegan butter
3–5 tablespoons water

MAKE AHEAD: Store the crackers in an airtight container in your pantry for up to 1 week.

MAKES | About 2½ cups
TOTAL TIME | 15 minutes
TOTAL COST | Under $10

The first time I made this, Adam and I devoured the entire bowl in approximately 30 seconds. So I made it again the next day, then the next day, then the next day. It takes only four ingredients to make the cheesy creamy queso sauce, then you just load it up with toppings. I love using a spicy salsa for extra punch, but this works well with whatever your favorite salsa is.

LOADED QUESO DIP

FOR THE QUESO DIP

½ cup raw cashews

1 cup red salsa (mild, medium, or spicy)

3 tablespoons nutritional yeast

¼ teaspoon turmeric

1–4 tablespoons water

FOR THE TOPPINGS

½ cup black beans, drained and rinsed, divided

½ cup corn kernels (thawed if frozen), divided

2 tablespoons roughly chopped fresh cilantro

½ jalapeño, sliced (optional)

Tortilla chips, for serving

1. If you do not have a high-powered blender, in a small pot, cover the cashews with water and boil for 10 minutes or until tender. Drain and rinse. If you have a high-powered blender, it will be strong enough to blend the cashews until smooth, so you can skip this first step.

2. Add the cashews, salsa, nutritional yeast, and turmeric to a blender and blend until completely smooth and creamy. If needed, add water 1 tablespoon at a time to thin it out until the desired consistency is reached.

3. You can serve the queso dip hot or cold. If you want to heat it (my personal preference), pour it into a heatproof bowl and microwave on high for 2–3 minutes, or heat in a small pot on the stove until warm.

4. Stir ¼ cup black beans and ¼ cup corn into the dip, then use the remaining black beans and corn to garnish the top, along with the cilantro and jalapeño, if using. Serve with tortilla chips.

MAKE AHEAD: You can make the queso ahead of time (steps 1–2) and store in an airtight container in the fridge for up to 3 days. When ready to serve, heat if desired, and add toppings.

SERVES | 1 per jar
TOTAL TIME | 15 minutes
COST PER JAR | $1–$5
(depending on your choices)

Making your own instant ramen may seem tricky, but it's as simple as shoving stuff in a jar and then popping the jars in the fridge for later. When ready to eat, fill the jar with boiling water and let steep, then enjoy. This is a great way to use up those small amounts of leftover veggies so that they don't go to waste. I like lining up four to five jars at a time and making a bunch of different soups so that I have lunch ready to go for a few days in a row. Take this to work and don't be surprised when your coworkers ask you how to make their own too.

DIY INSTANT RAMEN SOUP

QUICK TIPS: 1. Check the cooking time of your noodles. If they take 3 minutes or less to boil, you can shove them straight into the jar without precooking them. **2.** If you use a store-bought vegetable broth powder, you may need to add more or less of the powder depending on how concentrated the mix is. Follow the package directions and use enough to make 1 cup of broth.

FOR THE RAMEN SOUP BASE

1 teaspoon Veggie Broth Powder (page 39 or store-bought, see Quick Tip)

1 teaspoon soy sauce (gluten-free if preferred)

⅛ teaspoon crushed red pepper flakes or ½ teaspoon Sriracha (optional for spice)

VEGGIES (½–1 CUP, ANY COMBO)

Mushrooms, thinly sliced

Carrots, peeled and grated or thinly sliced

Bell peppers, thinly sliced

Peas, fresh or frozen

Corn kernels, fresh or frozen

Baby corn, cut in chunks

Baby spinach leaves

Finely chopped kale

Cabbage, thinly sliced

Tofu, cubed

Shelled edamame, fresh or frozen

NOODLES (½–1 CUP, CHOOSE 1, SEE QUICK TIP)

Cooked ramen

Cooked udon

Dry rice vermicelli

Dry instant noodles

FLAVOR BOOSTERS (AS MANY AS YOU LIKE)

1 green onion, sliced

1 small handful fresh cilantro, roughly chopped

¼ cup bean sprouts

1 lime wedge

2 tablespoons peanuts

1 tablespoon sesame seeds

Small packets of soy sauce or hot sauce

MAKE AHEAD: Follow step 1 to prepare as many jars as you like. Store the sealed jars in the fridge for up to 5 days. Proceed with step 2 when ready to enjoy!

---

1. Add the veggie broth powder, soy sauce, and pepper flakes, if desired, to the bottom of a sealable, heatproof, 16-ounce jar. Add the veggies, followed by the noodles. Use a small bag or square of parchment paper to separate the flavor boosters from the noodles, then place flavor boosters on top and seal the jar. (Alternatively, you can store the flavor boosters in a separate small container.)

2. When ready to enjoy, remove the flavor boosters, fill the jar with boiling water, and reseal. Let steep for 3–5 minutes, until the noodles are tender. Stir everything together, then add the flavor boosters and enjoy!

SERVES | 6–8

TOTAL TIME | 30 minutes

TOTAL COST | Under $7

This classic soup is loaded with veggies, beans, and pasta in a flavorful broth, making it seem like you spent hours preparing it. I have a secret: it's a surprisingly simple one-pot meal! One of my little hacks in this recipe is to cook the pasta straight in the soup. Not only does this save time and extra dishes, but the starch from the pasta thickens the broth slightly for a more luscious soup. Serve minestrone with a crusty loaf of bread and a nice glass of red wine.

30-MINUTE MINESTRONE

1 tablespoon olive oil

2 medium carrots, peeled and chopped

1 yellow onion, chopped

4 cloves garlic, minced or pressed

4 cups vegetable broth

1 can (28 ounces) diced tomatoes (about 3⅓ cups)

2 teaspoons Italian Seasoning (page 48 or store-bought)

½ teaspoon salt

¼ teaspoon black pepper

1½ cups uncooked small pasta noodles, such as macaroni or ditalini (gluten-free if preferred, see Quick Tip)

1 can (19 ounces) red kidney beans, drained and rinsed (about 2 cups)

1½ cups chopped fresh or frozen green beans

1. Heat the oil in a large stockpot over medium-high heat, then add the carrots, onions, and garlic. Sauté for about 5 minutes, until the vegetables soften and begin to brown.

2. Add the broth, tomatoes, Italian seasoning, salt, and pepper. Cover and bring to a light boil, cooking for about 5 minutes, until the tomatoes are cooked. Add the pasta and kidney beans, cover, and cook for 5–10 minutes more, until the pasta is al dente. Stir in the green beans and heat through, about 1 minute. Serve hot.

QUICK TIP: If using a pasta other than traditional wheat, you might want to cook the pasta separately, drain, then add it to the soup. Some types of pasta, such as rice pasta, can make the soup slimy, so we want to avoid this.

MAKE AHEAD: Once cooled, store the soup in an airtight container in the fridge for up to 3 days. Leftover soup may result in the pasta absorbing a lot of the broth. To thin it out, just add water or more broth to reach the desired consistency.

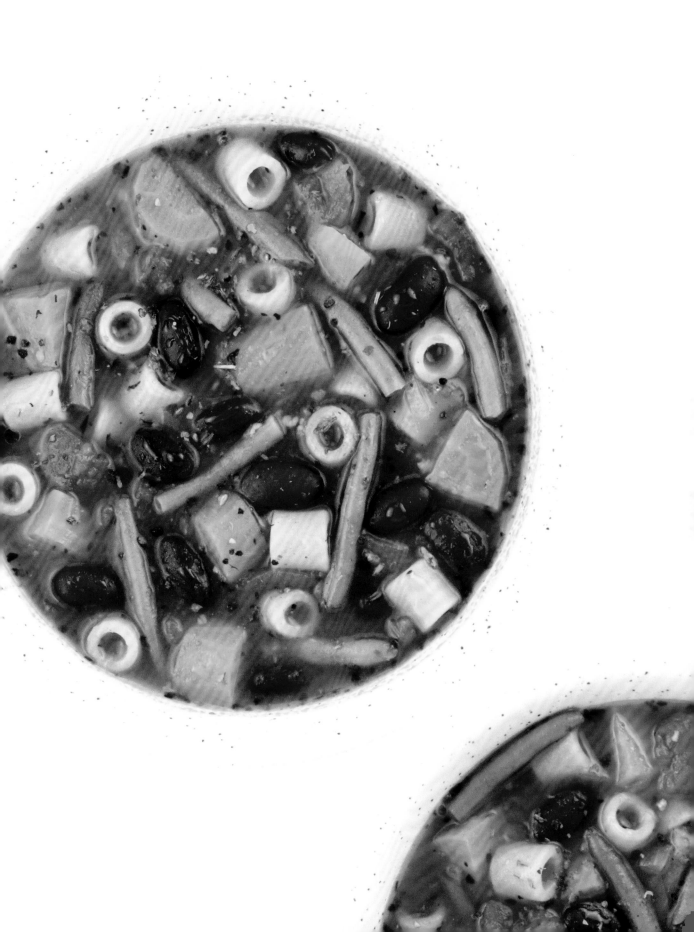

Sometimes I'm too lazy to go to the grocery store, so I try to make recipes work with what I have. I always seem to have a bag of carrots lingering somewhere in the back corner of my fridge, and a can of coconut milk in the cupboard, so this soup has become a too-lazy-to-shop staple. Not a fan of curry? No problem—skip the curry powder in this recipe for a simple soup that will still satisfy.

SERVES | 4
TOTAL TIME | 30 minutes
TOTAL COST | Under $5

CURRY COCONUT CARROT SOUP

1. Heat the oil in a large pot over medium-high heat. When hot, add the carrots, onions, and garlic and sauté for about 5 minutes, until the onions turn translucent and begin to brown.

2. Add the vegetable broth, curry powder (if using), salt, and pepper and cover, then bring to a simmer. Continue to simmer until carrots are fork-tender and will blend easily, about 15 minutes. Once soft, add the coconut milk and use an immersion blender or standing blender to blend the soup until it is smooth and creamy. If using a standing blender, be careful not to overfill the blender; you may need to blend in batches.

3. Return the soup to the pot (if using a standing blender). Bring back to a simmer and serve hot.

1 tablespoon olive oil or vegan butter

2 cups peeled and chopped carrots (about 1 pound)

1 yellow onion, chopped

3 cloves garlic, minced

2 cups vegetable broth

1 teaspoon curry powder (optional)

¼ teaspoon salt

¼ teaspoon black pepper

1 cup full-fat coconut milk

QUICK TIP: The smaller you chop the carrots, the faster they will cook. This is a great time to use a food processor, if you have one, to speed up the chopping. You could even grate the carrots for a superfast-cooking soup.

MAKE AHEAD: Once the soup has cooled it can be stored in an airtight container in the fridge for up to 4 days or in the freezer for up to 3 months.

Please sir/ma'am/friend/genius cook, may I have some more? These are words you will most likely hear when you make this soup. It's so creamy-rich delicious, and the gnocchi make it filling enough to be a meal in itself. I'm all about the chewy bite of the gnocchi in this soup, but if you like, you can sub a short pasta such as shells, orecchiette, or macaroni (gluten-free if preferred). If you do so, note that the pasta may take a little longer to cook in the soup.

SERVES | 6
TOTAL TIME | 30 minutes
TOTAL COST | Under $10

CREAMY GNOCCHI SOUP

1. Heat the oil in a large pot over medium-high heat. Add the carrots, celery, onions, and garlic and sauté for about 5 minutes, until the onions turn translucent and begin to brown.

2. Sprinkle the flour over the vegetables and continue to cook for 1 minute while stirring often. Pour the broth into the pot and use your spoon to scrape up any bits stuck to the bottom of the pan. Add the seasoning, salt, and pepper and bring to a simmer.

3. Gently stir in the gnocchi and continue to cook for 3–5 minutes, until the gnocchi are tender. Finally, add the plant-based milk and spinach and cook for another 1–2 minutes, until heated through and the spinach is wilted. Serve hot.

MAKE AHEAD: Let the soup cool before storing in an airtight container in the fridge for up to 3 days.

2 tablespoons olive oil

2 medium carrots, peeled and chopped

2 stalks celery, chopped

1 yellow onion, chopped

4 cloves garlic, minced or pressed

¼ cup all-purpose flour (gluten-free if preferred)

4 cups vegetable broth

2 teaspoons Italian Seasoning (page 48 or store-bought)

¾ teaspoon salt

¼ teaspoon black pepper

1 package (1 pound) prepared gnocchi (check to make sure it's vegan, gluten-free if preferred)

2 cups plant-based milk, such as oat or soy

2 handfuls fresh spinach (about 4 cups)

SERVES | 4
TOTAL TIME | 15 minutes
TOTAL COST | Under $10

This soup is so beyond easy—it takes less than 15 minutes to make (no, really). But don't be fooled into thinking that the speediness of this soup means you'll be sacrificing flavor. Spicy jalapeño, zesty lime, and hearty beans topped with creamy avocado and the salty crunch of tortilla chips—this is about as flavorful as it gets.

15-MINUTE LIME & BEAN SOUP

1 tablespoon light oil, such as canola or vegetable

1 yellow onion, finely chopped

½–1 jalapeño, finely chopped

6 cloves garlic, minced or pressed

4 cups vegetable broth

1 can (19 ounces) large white beans (lima or fava beans work well), drained and rinsed (about 2 cups)

Juice of 1 lime (about 2 tablespoons)

1½ teaspoons Tacos & More Seasoning (page 48 or store-bought taco seasoning)

½ teaspoon salt

2 avocados, peeled, pitted, and sliced, for garnish

½ cup chopped fresh cilantro, for garnish

Tortilla chips, for serving

1. In a large pot, heat the oil over medium-high heat, then add the onions, jalapeños (add more or less to suit spice preference), and garlic and sauté until the onions turn translucent and begin to brown, about 5 minutes.

2. Add the broth, beans, lime juice, taco seasoning, and salt. Bring to a light boil and cook for 5 minutes. Divide soup among bowls and garnish with avocado and cilantro. Serve a bowl of tortilla chips on the side and encourage everyone to crush some chips into their bowl of soup for a little added crunch.

MAKE AHEAD: Store the cooled soup in an airtight container in the fridge for up to 3 days or in the freezer for up to 3 months. Garnish with fresh toppings when you serve.

This creamy veggie-packed soup is the perfect way to hide away from rainy days. It has all the comforting flavors of a classic pot pie, but without any of the hassle of making or working with pie crust. Serve it with a crusty loaf of bread, soda crackers, or homemade biscuits (page 30).

SERVES | 4–6
TOTAL TIME | 30 minutes
TOTAL COST | Under $7

PERFECT POT-PIE SOUP

1. Melt the butter in a large pot over medium-high heat, then add the carrots, onions, and garlic. Sauté the veggies for about 5 minutes, until they begin to soften.

2. Sprinkle the flour over the veggies and cook for 1 minute more. Stir in the broth, potatoes, thyme, salt, and pepper. Bring to a simmer and cook for 5–10 minutes, until the vegetables are cooked and the soup has thickened slightly. Add the plant-based milk and peas and heat through, another 2–3 minutes. Serve hot.

MAKE AHEAD: Store the cooled soup in an airtight container in the fridge for up to 3 days or in the freezer for up to 3 months.

2 tablespoons vegan butter

2 medium carrots, peeled and chopped

1 yellow onion, chopped

3 cloves garlic, minced or pressed

6 tablespoons all-purpose flour (gluten-free if preferred)

4 cups vegetable broth

2 medium Yukon gold potatoes (about 1 pound), peeled and finely diced

2 teaspoons dried thyme leaves

1½ teaspoons salt

½ teaspoon black pepper

1½ cups plant-based milk, such as soy or oat

1 cup fresh or frozen peas

SERVES | 4–6
TOTAL TIME | 25 minutes
TOTAL COST | Under $5

Don't throw out those bread ends or stale slices of bread, use them in this soup! The bread soaks up the broth and softens, then can be easily blended, which takes the soup from thin and boring to rich, thick, and creamy. Save the leftovers because this garlic-infused soup is even better the next day.

GARLIC BREAD SOUP

FOR THE GARLIC BREAD SOUP

1 tablespoon vegan butter

1 yellow onion, chopped

8 cloves garlic, pressed or minced

4 cups vegetable broth

5 slices bread, cubed (4 cups, gluten-free if preferred)

2 cups plant-based milk, such as oat or soy

1 teaspoon Italian Seasoning (page 48 or store-bought)

¾ teaspoon salt

½ teaspoon black pepper

1 handful fresh parsley, chopped, for garnish (optional)

FOR THE GARLIC BREAD CROUTONS (OPTIONAL)

2 tablespoons vegan butter

3 slices bread, cubed (2½ cups, gluten-free if preferred)

2 cloves garlic, pressed or minced

¼ teaspoon salt

1. To make the soup, melt the butter in a large pot over medium-high heat. Add the onions and garlic and sauté until the onions turn translucent and begin to brown, about 5 minutes. Pour in the broth and use your spoon to scrape off any bits stuck to the bottom of the pan. Add the bread cubes, plant-based milk, seasoning, salt, and pepper.

2. Bring the soup to a simmer and cook until the bread is completely softened, 5–10 minutes. Use an immersion blender or standing blender to blend the soup until completely smooth. If using a standing blender, you may want to blend the soup in batches to avoid overfilling the blender.

3. Return the soup to the pot (if using a standing blender) and heat through.

4. To make the croutons (if using), melt the butter in a skillet or frying pan. Add the bread, garlic, and salt. Stir frequently until the bread cubes have turned golden and crispy. Remove from heat.

5. Serve the soup by ladling into bowls and topping with the croutons and parsley (if using) for garnish.

MAKE AHEAD: Store leftover soup and croutons separately. Croutons can be stored in an airtight container in the pantry. Allow the soup to cool and store in an airtight container in the fridge for up to 3 days or in the freezer for up to 3 months.

When I first made this soup, I scooped a little spoonful straight from the pot to test it. My eyes popped wide open, and I immediately ladled a generous serving into the nearest bowl I could reach, then proceeded to gobble down the soup at record speed. Creamy and rich, with sweet pops of corn and a zing of jalapeño, this dish is truly something special. If sweet and spicy is a flavor combination you enjoy, you are gonna go crazy for this soup!

SERVES | 6–8
TOTAL TIME | 21 minutes
TOTAL COST | Under $10

NO-SWEAT SWEET ⁚ SPICY CORN SOUP

1. In a large pot, heat the oil over medium-high heat. When hot, add the red peppers, onions, garlic, and the finely chopped jalapeños and sauté until the onions turn translucent and begin to brown.

2. Sprinkle the flour over the vegetables and stir as the flour cooks for about 1 minute. Add the corn and vegetable broth. Bring to a simmer and cook for about 5 minutes, stirring often, until the soup is creamy and slightly thickened. Lastly, stir in the coconut milk and remove from the heat.

3. Divide among bowls and garnish with the remaining sliced jalapeño.

QUICK TIP: Coconut is my preference for making soups creamy, but you can sub another plant-based milk if you prefer. Just make sure the one you choose is high in fat, such as cashew cream (page 18), so it maintains richness and won't separate.

MAKE AHEAD: Allow the soup to cool before storing in an airtight container in the fridge for up to 3 days or in the freezer for up to 3 months.

---

1 tablespoon light oil, such as canola or vegetable

1 red bell pepper, chopped

1 yellow onion, chopped

4 cloves garlic, minced or pressed

2 jalapeños, 1 finely chopped and 1 sliced, for garnish

3 tablespoons all-purpose flour (gluten-free if preferred)

6 cups (26 ounces) fresh or frozen corn kernels

4 cups vegetable broth

1 can (14 fluid ounces) full-fat coconut milk (about 1¾ cups)

2 teaspoons Tacos & More Seasoning (page 48 or store-bought taco seasoning)

This classic salad is a cinch to make but satisfies every time. Broccoli florets are coated in a creamy and tangy dressing, dried cranberries add a pop of sweetness, and roasted salted sunflower seeds provide a little extra oomph. You can whip this up last minute, but it's also great made ahead of time—the flavors will intensify as it sits, making it a perfect potluck dish.

SERVES | 6 as a side
TOTAL TIME | 15 minutes
TOTAL COST | Under $7

BRISK BROCCOLI SALAD

1. In a large bowl, mix the mayonnaise, vinegar, garlic, and pepper to combine.

2. Add the broccoli, onions, dried cranberries, and sunflower seeds to the mayonnaise dressing. Toss well until everything is evenly coated with the dressing. Enjoy fresh or store for later.

MAKE AHEAD: Cover and store the salad in the fridge for up to 2 days.

½ cup vegan mayonnaise

2 tablespoons apple cider vinegar

2 cloves garlic, minced or pressed

¼ teaspoon black pepper

1 large head broccoli (12 ounces), chopped into bite-size pieces (about 4 cups)

½ cup chopped red onions

½ cup dried cranberries

½ cup roasted salted sunflower seeds

SERVES | 2–4
TOTAL TIME | 15 minutes
TOTAL COST | Under $10

Don't be fooled by the simple ingredients in this salad—it's bursting with crunch and zing. This makes for a great lunch or lazy supper, or it can be served as a side to my DIY Instant Ramen Soup (page 98) or Get 'er Done Garlic Noodles (page 134) for a sensational feast.

QUICK CRUNCHY CABBAGE SALAD

1 head napa cabbage or bok choy (12 ounces), chopped

1 carrot, peeled and grated

½ cup sliced almonds or roughly chopped peanuts

1 tablespoon sesame seeds

1 batch Sesame Dressing (page 129)

1. Add all the ingredients to a large bowl along with the prepared dressing. Toss well to evenly coat the salad, and serve fresh.

Loaded with hearty chickpeas and sweet, crispy pops of apple, this salad is a lunchtime favorite in my house. It's great served on its own, or even loaded up on a slice of bread or wrapped in a tortilla for a fantastic sandwich.

SERVES | 2 as a main, 4 as a side
TOTAL TIME | 15 minutes
TOTAL COST | Under $7

15-MINUTE APPLE CHICKPEA SALAD

1. Add the chickpeas, apples, celery, onions, and raisins to a large bowl. Toss to combine, drizzle with the dressing to taste, and then toss again to coat.

MAKE AHEAD: This salad will store well covered in the fridge for 4–5 days.

1 can (19 ounces) chickpeas, drained and rinsed (about 2 cups)

1 apple (any kind), chopped

2 stalks celery, thinly sliced

¼ red onion, chopped

¼ cup raisins

1 batch Maple Dijon Dressing (page 129)

Imagine this: you go to a potluck or barbecue and pop this salad on the table. It looks good, so the guests give it a try, and then the magic happens. Creamy, zesty, sweet, and smoky, this isn't any regular old salad, this is wizardry, they realize! You better believe a hefty second helping of this corn salad will appear on everyone's plates.

SERVES | 6 as a side
TOTAL TIME | 10 minutes
TOTAL COST | Under $7

10-MINUTE ZESTY CORN SALAD

1. Add the corn, onions, avocados, cilantro, and jalapeños to a large bowl. Toss to combine, then drizzle with the dressing to taste, and toss again to combine.

MAKE AHEAD: This salad stores well covered in the fridge for up to 3 days. The avocados might brown a bit, so you can chop and add them just before serving, if you'd like fresh green avocados in the salad.

3 cups cooked corn kernels (thawed frozen kernels work great)

¼ red onion, chopped

1 avocado, peeled, pitted, and chopped

1 handful fresh cilantro, chopped (about ⅓ cup)

½–1 jalapeño, finely chopped

1 batch Smoky Lime Dressing (page 130)

SERVES | 2 as a main,
4 as a side

TOTAL TIME | 20 minutes

TOTAL COST | Under $7

I don't know what it is, but whenever there's a kale Caesar salad on the menu, I have to order it. The tangy, creamy dressing combined with the hearty chew of kale is a love affair I just can't get enough of. I hacked up this recipe to make it super simple and quick to prepare so that I can enjoy it whenever I like, no restaurant needed. I use both kale and romaine for the best crunchy-chewy combo, toss the greens in a cheater Caesar salad dressing (using hummus as the base), and top with homemade three-ingredient croutons. Hello, easy deliciousness.

QUICK KALE CAESAR

FOR THE CROUTONS

2 tablespoons olive oil

3 slices bread, cut into small cubes (about 2½ cups, gluten-free if preferred)

1 tablespoon Tacos & More Seasoning (page 48 or store-bought taco seasoning, see Quick Tip)

FOR THE SALAD

3 cups destemmed and finely sliced kale

3 cups roughly chopped romaine lettuce

1 batch Hummus Caesar Dressing (page 130)

1. To make the croutons, heat the oil in a large skillet over medium-high heat. When hot, add the bread cubes and seasoning and stir to evenly coat. Cook until the bread is toasted and golden all over, about 5 minutes. Set aside.

2. Add the kale and romaine to a large bowl and dress with the Caesar dressing, to taste. Toss very well to coat. Top with the croutons.

QUICK TIP: You can sub the Tacos & More Seasoning for equal amounts of Italian Seasoning (page 48) or Cajun Seasoning (page 49) for other crouton flavor options.

This salad is a double whammy of marinated artichokes. You get the artichokes themselves, but the dressing is made with the leftover liquid from the jar of artichokes. The white beans turn this salad from a side dish to a heartier main, but feel free to skip them or sub with vegan croutons for a lightened-up variation.

ASAP ARTICHOKE SALAD

6 cups baby spinach leaves

1 can (19 ounces) white beans, such as kidney or lima, drained and rinsed (about 2 cups)

1 jar (6 ounces) marinated artichoke hearts, chopped (use leftover liquid in Artichoke Dressing)

1 large tomato, cut into wedges

¼ red onion, thinly sliced

1 batch Artichoke Dressing (page 131)

1. Add the spinach, white beans, artichoke hearts, tomato wedges, and red onions to a large bowl. Drizzle the dressing overtop to taste, and lightly toss to coat.

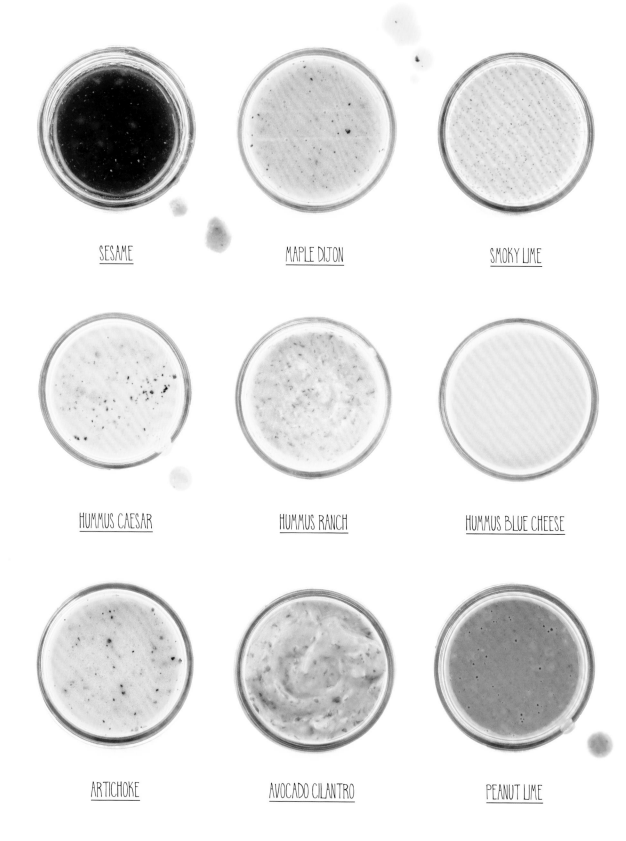

SESAME MAPLE DIJON SMOKY LIME

HUMMUS CAESAR HUMMUS RANCH HUMMUS BLUE CHEESE

ARTICHOKE AVOCADO CILANTRO PEANUT LIME

Do not underestimate the power of a good sauce! My fridge is always bursting with jars of homemade dressings and sauces for one main reason: they make everything taste amazing! If a dish is ever seeming a bit plain, just drizzle a little dressing overtop for an instant amp-up. Some of these dressings are called for in other recipes (don't worry, the combined recipes will still total 10 ingredients or less). Other dressings you can use wherever you please, like on a Guzinta Bowl (page 190).

DRESSINGS & SAUCES

SESAME DRESSING

MAKES: ABOUT ¼ CUP | TOTAL TIME: 5 MINUTES | TOTAL COST: UNDER $3

Add all the ingredients to a sealable jar. Shake well to combine. Store in an airtight container in the fridge for up to 1 week.

2 tablespoons soy sauce (gluten-free if preferred)

1 tablespoon rice vinegar or lime juice

1 tablespoon agave or corn syrup

1 teaspoon sesame oil

1 clove garlic, minced or pressed

¼ teaspoon ground ginger

MAPLE DIJON DRESSING

MAKES: ABOUT ½ CUP | TOTAL TIME: 5 MINUTES | TOTAL COST: UNDER $3

Add all the ingredients to a sealable jar and shake well to combine. Store in an airtight container in the fridge for up to 1 week.

2 tablespoons olive oil

2 tablespoons maple syrup or agave

2 tablespoons Dijon mustard

2 tablespoons lemon juice

¼ teaspoon garlic powder

¼ teaspoon salt

¼ teaspoon black pepper

recipe continues

3 tablespoons vegan
mayonnaise

3 tablespoons lime juice

1 clove garlic, minced
or pressed

½ teaspoon smoked paprika

¼ teaspoon salt

SMOKY LIME DRESSING

MAKES: ABOUT ⅓ CUP | TOTAL TIME: 5 MINUTES | TOTAL COST: UNDER $3

Add all the ingredients to a sealable jar and shake well to combine.
This will keep fresh for up to 5 days when kept in an airtight
container in the fridge.

¼ cup prepared hummus

1 tablespoon lemon juice

1 tablespoon nutritional yeast

1 teaspoon capers, finely
minced

1 teaspoon brine from caper
jar

1 teaspoon Dijon mustard

1 clove garlic, finely minced

¼ teaspoon black pepper

½–2 tablespoons water

HUMMUS CAESAR DRESSING

MAKES: ABOUT ⅓ CUP | TOTAL TIME: 5 MINUTES | TOTAL COST: UNDER $3

In a small bowl, whisk together the hummus, lemon juice, nutritional
yeast, capers, caper brine, mustard, garlic, and pepper until combined
and creamy. Add water, as needed, to thin the dressing to the desired
consistency. Store in an airtight container in the fridge for up to 5 days.

½ cup prepared hummus

4 teaspoons apple cider
vinegar

1 teaspoon dried parsley

1 teaspoon dried chives

¾ teaspoon onion powder

½ teaspoon dried dill

½ teaspoon garlic powder

2 tablespoons water
(or as needed)

HUMMUS RANCH DRESSING

MAKES: ABOUT ⅓ CUP | TOTAL TIME: 5 MINUTES | TOTAL COST: UNDER $3

In a small bowl, whisk together the hummus, vinegar, dried parsley,
dried chives, onion powder, dried dill, and garlic powder until
combined. Add the water, as needed, to thin to a dressing
consistency. The dressing will keep fresh for up to 5 days when
stored in the fridge in an airtight container.

¼ cup prepared hummus

2 tablespoons nutritional yeast

1 tablespoon white miso paste

2 teaspoons apple cider
vinegar

½ teaspoon onion powder

½–2 tablespoons water
(or as needed)

HUMMUS BLUE CHEESE DRESSING

MAKES: ABOUT ⅓ CUP | TOTAL TIME: 5 MINUTES | TOTAL COST: UNDER $3

In a small bowl, whisk together the hummus, nutritional yeast, miso,
vinegar, and onion powder until smooth. Add the water, as needed, to
thin to the desired consistency. Store in an airtight container in the
fridge for up to 5 days.

ARTICHOKE DRESSING

MAKES: ABOUT ¾ CUP | TOTAL TIME: 5 MINUTES | TOTAL COST: UNDER $1

Add all the ingredients to a sealable jar and shake well to combine. The dressing will keep fresh in the fridge in an airtight container for up to 1 week.

- ½ cup marinated artichoke liquid (if there isn't enough, add olive oil to make ½ cup liquid)
- 2 tablespoons nutritional yeast
- 1 tablespoon Dijon mustard
- 1 teaspoon agave or maple syrup
- ¼ teaspoon black pepper

PEANUT LIME DRESSING

SERVES: ABOUT ⅓ CUP | TOTAL TIME: 5 MINUTES | TOTAL COST: UNDER $3

Add all the ingredients to a small bowl and whisk until well combined. Store in an airtight container in the fridge for up to 1 week.

- 2 tablespoons smooth natural peanut butter
- 2 tablespoons lime juice (about 1 lime)
- 1 tablespoon soy sauce (gluten-free if preferred)
- 1 teaspoon Sriracha (optional)
- 1 clove garlic, minced
- 1 teaspoon minced fresh ginger
- ½ teaspoon sesame oil

AVOCADO CILANTRO SAUCE

MAKES: ABOUT 1 CUP | TOTAL TIME: 5 MINUTES | TOTAL COST: UNDER $5

Add all the ingredients to a food processor or blender, and blend until your sauce is smooth. This dressing is best used fresh.

- 1 small avocado, peeled and pitted
- ½ cup fresh cilantro
- ¼ cup water
- 1 clove garlic
- 1 tablespoon lime juice
- 1 teaspoon agave or corn syrup
- ¼ teaspoon salt

SERVES | 4

TOTAL TIME | 15 minutes

TOTAL COST | Under $5

Garlic + noodles . . . what's not to love? These garlicky noodles are the perfect dinner for when you have nothing left in the fridge, as they're made almost entirely from pantry staples! These noodles are so simple, yet the flavors will have you slurping them down in record time.

GET 'ER DONE GARLIC NOODLES

8 ounces thin rice noodles or similar noodles (gluten-free if preferred)

¼ cup soy sauce (gluten-free if preferred)

¼ cup brown sugar

2 tablespoons rice vinegar

4 teaspoons sesame oil

3 tablespoons vegan butter

6 green onions, sliced, divided

8 cloves garlic, minced

1 tablespoon sesame seeds, for garnish

1. Bring a large pot of water to a boil and cook the noodles according to package directions.

2. In a small bowl, mix together the soy sauce, sugar, rice vinegar, and sesame oil, and set aside.

3. Melt the vegan butter in a large skillet over medium-high heat then add about two-thirds of the green onions and all of the garlic. Sauté for 1–3 minutes, until fragrant. Add the cooked noodles and the sauce. Toss well and heat through. Garnish with the remaining green onions and sesame seeds and serve hot.

QUICK TIP: If you have veggies or tofu on hand, feel free to chop them up and add them to this noodle dish. Bell peppers, carrots, broccoli, peas, and mushrooms all work well. Sauté the additional veg in the vegan butter until tender before adding the onions and garlic.

MAKE AHEAD: Store the cooled noodles in an airtight container in the fridge for up to 3 days.

This is like a BLT sandwich but made into a pasta salad! As always, the *L* stands for lettuce and the *T* for tomato, but the *B* in this recipe name is for spicy, buttery bread cubes. The crispy cubes with Cajun-inspired seasoning are so irresistible—just try to be polite and leave some of the cubes for other guests.

SERVES | 4 as a main, 8 as a side
TOTAL TIME | 30 minutes
TOTAL COST | Under $10

SPICED-UP BLT PASTA SALAD

1. Bring a large pot of water to a boil and cook pasta according to package directions. Drain the pasta and rinse well with cold water to cool the pasta completely.

2. In the meantime, heat a large skillet over medium-high heat and melt the vegan butter. Add the bread cubes and seasoning, stirring to coat the bread. Fry the bread until it's golden and crispy. Remove from the heat and set aside.

3. To a large bowl, add the cooled and drained pasta, tomatoes, lettuce, onions, mayonnaise, lemon juice, salt, and pepper. Toss well to combine. Scatter the toasted bread cubes on top and serve right away.

3½ cups short pasta, such as farfalle, shells, macaroni, or orecchiette (gluten-free if preferred)

2 tablespoons vegan butter

3 slices bread, cut into small cubes (about 2½ cups, gluten-free if preferred)

1 tablespoon Cajun Seasoning (page 49 or store-bought, see Quick Tip)

2 large tomatoes, cut into wedges

1 head romaine lettuce, chopped

¼ red onion, thinly sliced

¼ cup vegan mayonnaise

2 tablespoons lemon juice

¾ teaspoon salt

¼ teaspoon black pepper

QUICK TIPS: 1. To make your bread cubes extra-crispy, spread the cubes out on a baking sheet and let them sit out overnight before making this dish. They will dry out a bit, making them extra-crunchy! **2.** If you're not a fan of spicy food, either make my Cajun Seasoning without the cayenne or sub with Tacos & More Seasoning (page 48).

MAKE AHEAD: If making ahead of time, keep the bread cubes in a separate container in the pantry and the pasta salad in an airtight container in the fridge for up to 3 days. Add the bread cubes to the pasta just before serving so they don't get soggy.

Not only is ordering noodles for delivery expensive, but most of the time they're often lacking in veggies and are way too greasy. Not for me, thanks. Make noodle dishes at home in less time than it takes for the delivery to arrive, and enjoy a perfectly balanced dish that tastes way better than takeout. These lo mein noodles are simple, but completely addictive. The lightly sweet sauce with all that good veg will have even picky eaters diving in.

LOW-MAINTENANCE LO MEIN

8 ounces vegan lo mein noodles or spaghetti (gluten-free if preferred)

1 head broccoli (12 ounces), cut into florets (about 4 cups)

1 tablespoon sesame oil

8 ounces mushrooms, sliced

1 medium carrot, grated

3 cloves garlic, minced

1-inch piece fresh ginger, minced

¼ cup soy sauce (gluten-free if preferred)

2 tablespoons brown sugar

1. Bring a large pot of water to a boil and cook the noodles according to package directions. In the last 4 minutes of cooking, add the broccoli to the boiling water. If your noodles take 4 minutes or less to cook, add the broccoli first, then follow with the noodles for the time needed. Drain the noodles and broccoli and set aside.

2. Heat the sesame oil in a large skillet over medium-high heat. When the oil is hot, add the mushrooms and cook them until they brown and begin to release their juices, about 5 minutes. Add the carrots, garlic, and ginger and cook for about 2–3 minutes more, until fragrant.

3. Add the noodles, broccoli, soy sauce, and brown sugar to the skillet. Toss well to evenly coat and heat through. These are best served hot, but leftover cold noodles make for a yummy lunch.

MAKE AHEAD: Once cooled, store in an airtight container in the fridge for 2–3 days.

Meaty, rich mushrooms in a simple tomato sauce with lots of rosemary, onions, and garlic—the taste of Italy! This satisfying pasta is my Adam's favorite pasta ever. It might seem unusual to add an entire large can of tomato paste to a dish, but trust me on this one. It instantly adds so much tomatoey goodness without the need for simmering tomatoes down for hours!

**SERVES | ** 4
**TOTAL TIME | ** 25 minutes
**TOTAL COST | ** Under $10

25-MINUTE TASTE OF ITALY

1. Bring a large pot of water to a boil and cook the pasta according to package directions. Before draining the pasta, reserve ½ cup pasta water.

2. In a large skillet or pot, melt the vegan butter over medium-high heat. When melted, add the mushrooms, onions, rosemary, garlic, and red pepper flakes, if desired. Sauté for about 5 minutes, until the onions begin to brown and the mushrooms cook down and begin to release their juices.

3. Add the pasta water, tomato paste, and salt to the sautéed vegetables and mix together to combine. Add the pasta and toss well to coat. Serve hot.

QUICK TIP: I love the heartiness of portobellos, but feel free to use any other kind of mushroom (about 8 ounces), and cut into thick slices or large chunks.

14 ounces pasta of choice, such as fettuccini, spaghetti, or penne (gluten-free if preferred)

2 tablespoons vegan butter

4 portobello mushrooms, thickly sliced (see Quick Tip)

1 yellow onion, thinly sliced

2 tablespoons finely chopped fresh rosemary (4–6 sprigs)

3 cloves garlic, minced or pressed

½ teaspoon crushed red pepper flakes (optional)

½ cup pasta water

1 can (13 ounces) tomato paste (about 1½ cups)

¾ teaspoon salt

Traditional gnocchi often contain eggs, but I was delighted to discover that most of the store-bought packages of gnocchi are accidentally vegan! These little potato-based pasta nuggets are gorgeously tender and completely luscious simmered in this creamy sauce. Finish off the dish with a handful of fresh basil and you will feel like you just ordered yourself a five-star dish at a one-star price.

10-INGREDIENT CREAMY BASIL GNOCCHI

2 tablespoons vegan butter

6 cloves garlic, minced or pressed

2 tablespoons all-purpose flour (gluten-free if preferred)

2½ cups plant-based milk, such as soy or oat

1 tablespoon nutritional yeast

2 teaspoons Dijon mustard

¾ teaspoon salt

¼ teaspoon black pepper, plus more for garnish

1 package (1 pound) prepared gnocchi (check to make sure it's vegan, see Quick Tip)

1 large handful fresh basil leaves, sliced or torn, plus more for garnish (see Quick Tip)

1. Heat the butter in a large skillet or pot over medium-high heat. Add the garlic and sauté for about 30 seconds, stirring continuously until fragrant. Sprinkle the flour into the pan and whisk into the butter and garlic to form a paste. Let cook for another 30 seconds while whisking, then whisk in the plant-based milk, nutritional yeast, mustard, salt, and pepper. Bring to a simmer and let cook for about 5 minutes until the sauce begins to thicken.

2. Add the gnocchi and let cook in the sauce for 3–4 minutes or until the gnocchi is fork-tender. Lastly, stir in the basil to wilt into the sauce, about 30 seconds. Serve hot with some fresh basil for garnish and a crack of pepper.

QUICK TIPS: 1. Try subbing in a few large handfuls of baby arugula for the basil for a completely different flavor combo. **2.** Not into gnocchi? Instead, boil up 1 pound of your favorite pasta (gluten-free if preferred) according to the package directions and toss that in the sauce.

MAKE AHEAD: You can make the sauce (step 1) ahead of time and store in an airtight container in the fridge for 1–2 days. When reheating the sauce, add a splash of extra water if needed to loosen, and continue with step 2.

Miso paste isn't just for soup. I love to use the rich umami taste to add an aged flavor to vegan cheeses and sauces, but here I use it as the mouthwatering base of a noodle dish. You may be surprised by just how creamy and rich these udon noodles become. Have fun slurping them up as is, or feel free to add some fresh or sautéed chopped vegetables.

SERVES | 4–6
TOTAL TIME | 10 minutes
TOTAL COST | Under $7

10-MINUTE CREAMY MISO UDON NOODLES

1. Bring a large pot of water to a boil and cook the udon noodles according to package directions, then drain the noodles.

2. In the meantime, heat the sesame oil in a large skillet or frying pan. When hot, add the garlic and ginger and cook for about 1 minute, until fragrant. Whisk in ½ cup water, miso paste, sugar, and lime zest and juice.

3. Add the cooked udon noodles to the sauce and toss well to coat. If the sauce is too thick, add up to ¼ cup more water as needed. Garnish with the green onions and sesame seeds. Serve hot.

14 ounces udon noodles (or 7 ounces of a dry noodle)

1 tablespoon sesame oil

2 cloves garlic, minced or pressed

1-inch piece fresh ginger, minced

½–¾ cup water

¼ cup white miso paste

1 tablespoon brown sugar

Zest and juice of 1 lime

6 green onions, chopped, for garnish

1 tablespoon sesame seeds, for garnish

MAKE AHEAD: Allow the noodles to cool before storing in an airtight container in the fridge for up to 3 days.

SERVES | 4

TOTAL TIME | 25 minutes

TOTAL COST | Under $10

Adding beans to pasta makes it an extra-satiating meal, so this is the perfect pasta on those super hungry days. Tossed in an aromatic, creamy sauce with sun-dried tomatoes and spinach, this is the stuff that pasta dreams are made of!

TUSCAN BEAN PASTA

14 ounces pasta of choice, such as spaghetti, penne, or rotini

1 tablespoon oil from jar of sun-dried tomatoes

1 yellow onion, chopped

4 cloves garlic, minced or pressed

¼ cup all-purpose flour (gluten-free if preferred)

2½ cups plant-based milk, such as soy or oat

2 teaspoons Italian Seasoning (page 48 or store-bought)

1 teaspoon salt

½ teaspoon black pepper

1 can (19 ounces) white beans, such as kidney or navy, drained and rinsed (about 2 cups)

½ jar (½ cup) sun-dried tomatoes, chopped (use leftover oil above)

3 cups baby spinach

2 tablespoons–½ cup reserved pasta water

1. Bring a large pot of water to a boil and cook the pasta according to package directions. Before draining the pasta, reserve ½ cup pasta water and set aside.

2. In the meantime, heat the oil in a large skillet or pot over medium-high heat. Add the onions and garlic and sauté for about 5 minutes, until they begin to brown.

3. Stir in the flour and cook for about 1 minute. Pour in the plant-based milk, Italian seasoning, salt, and pepper and whisk well. Cook the sauce until thickened, about 5 more minutes, then stir in the white beans, sun-dried tomatoes, and spinach. Cook until heated through and the spinach has wilted, 2–5 minutes more.

4. Add the hot pasta and a splash of the reserved pasta water to thin if needed. Serve hot.

MAKE AHEAD: Store the cooled pasta in an airtight container in the fridge for up to 3 days.

Even I admit it: unseasoned vegetables can be boring. But when you sauté up veg with garlic, onions, and Cajun-inspired spices, they turn from bland into spicy rich treasures of flavor. Get your fork ready to dig for the gold in this fiery pasta.

SERVES | 4
TOTAL TIME | 25 minutes
TOTAL COST | Under $10

CAJUN-SPICED VEGGIE PASTA

1. Bring a large pot of water to a boil and cook the pasta according to package directions. Before draining the pasta, reserve ½ cup pasta water and set aside.

2. Add the almonds to a small dry frying pan and set over medium heat. Toast the almonds until they just begin to brown, shaking the pan as needed. Remove from heat and set aside.

3. In a large skillet, heat the oil over medium-high heat. When hot, add the mushrooms, zucchini, onions, and garlic. Cook for about 10 minutes, until the veggies begin to brown. Stir in the tomatoes, Cajun seasoning, and ¼ cup reserved pasta water and heat through for 2 minutes more.

4. Add the pasta and toss well, adding the remaining ¼ cup pasta water if needed to help the sauce coat the noodles. Garnish with toasted almonds.

14 ounces short pasta, such as cavatappi, penne, or rigatoni (gluten-free if preferred)

¼ cup roughly chopped almonds

1 tablespoon olive oil

8 ounces button mushrooms, sliced

2 medium zucchini, sliced

1 red onion, thickly sliced

2 cloves garlic, minced or pressed

1 cup halved grape tomatoes

1 tablespoon Cajun Seasoning (page 49 or store-bought)

¼–½ cup reserved pasta water

MAKE AHEAD: Once cooled, the pasta can be stored in an airtight container in the fridge for up to 3 days.

SERVES | 4

TOTAL TIME | 20 minutes

TOTAL COST | Under $7

Avocados aren't just for guacamole or fancy toast. When you blend them up with fresh basil and garlic, you have an instantly creamy and rich pesto-inspired sauce. Toss it with hot pasta for a super quick and mouthwatering meal. Be sure to eat this one fresh, as avocados tend to brown when they sit out for a while (so it won't make for great leftovers).

PRESTO AVOCADO PESTO

14 ounces spaghetti or similar pasta (gluten-free if preferred)

2 ripe avocados, peeled and pitted

1 large handful fresh basil leaves (about 2 cups/ 1 ounce)

2 cloves garlic

Zest and juice of 1 lemon

1 teaspoon salt

½ teaspoon black pepper

1. Bring a large pot of water to a boil and cook pasta according to package directions.

2. Meanwhile, add the avocados, basil, garlic, lemon juice, salt, and pepper to a food processor or blender. Process until smooth and creamy. If you don't have a food processor or blender, simply mince or press the garlic first and finely chop the basil, then mash everything together in a bowl with a fork.

3. Toss the avocado basil sauce with the hot pasta and garnish with lemon zest. Serve hot.

SERVES | 4
TOTAL TIME | 15 minutes
TOTAL COST | $5–$10
(depending on your choices)

While I love making a homemade tomato sauce from scratch, sometimes I don't have the time, and other times I do have the time but am just feeling too lazy. We've all been there, right? Grocery store shelves are full of different pasta sauces, but many of them aren't vegan, leaving mostly just the plain sauce for us animal-free-food lovers. Plain tomato sauce is fine, but use this guide to easily amp up your jar of tomato sauce to something much more exciting!

TOMATO SAUCE AMPER-UPPERS

1 jar (20 ounces) store-bought tomato sauce
Cooked pasta of choice (gluten-free if preferred)

BEFORE THE SAUCE

1–4 tablespoons olive oil or vegan butter

1 onion, chopped

2–6 cloves garlic, minced

8 ounces sliced mushrooms

1–3 carrots, peeled and chopped

1–3 stalks celery, chopped

1 bell pepper, chopped

1–2 zucchini, chopped

WITH THE SAUCE

1–3 teaspoons Italian Seasoning (page 48 or store-bought)

¼–½ teaspoon crushed red pepper flakes or hot sauce

Fresh basil, roughly chopped

Fresh rosemary, chopped

Fresh thyme leaves, chopped

1–3 tablespoons chopped fresh parsley

¼ teaspoon liquid smoke or ½ teaspoon smoked paprika

1–3 tablespoons tomato paste

1–3 teaspoons white or brown sugar

2–4 teaspoons capers

¼–½ cup olives

¼–½ cup roughly chopped artichoke hearts

½–1 cup halved cherry or grape tomatoes

¼–½ cup pasta water

¼–½ cup chopped walnuts, toasted

¼–½ cup chopped sun-dried tomatoes

2 large handfuls greens, such as spinach, arugula, or chopped kale

QUICK TIP: If your tomato sauce already contains some of the suggested ingredients, it may seem redundant to add more, but fresh ingredients will enhance the sauce and make it taste and look freshly made.

MAKE AHEAD: Allow the sauce to cool before storing in an airtight container in the fridge for up to 3 days.

AFTER THE SAUCE (GARNISH TO TASTE)

Fresh basil leaves

Fresh parsley, chopped

Salt and black pepper

Crushed red pepper flakes

Nutritional yeast

Ground cashews, almonds, or macadamia nuts

Roasted and salted sunflower seeds

Roasted pine nuts

---

1. If cooking any of the "Before the Sauce" ingredients, heat the oil or vegan butter in a large skillet or pot over medium-high heat. Add any of the "Before the Sauce" ingredients. Choose one or as many as you'd like. Once the veggies are sautéed and beginning to brown, pour in the jar of tomato sauce.

2. You can now add any of the "With the Sauce" ingredients. Choose as many or as few of these additions as you'd like and heat the sauce through.

3. Once you are happy with your sauce, toss it with the cooked pasta of your choice or spoon over the pasta. Garnish with any of the "After the Sauce" ingredients.

recipe continues

ᵒ ᵒ

SOME OF MY FAVORITE COMBOS

Sun-dried Tomato: Tomato sauce, vegan butter, sun-dried tomatoes, arugula, and walnuts.

Olives & Capers: Tomato sauce, olives, capers, fresh thyme leaves, ground almonds, and nutritional yeast.

Zucchini & Garlic: Tomato sauce, olive oil, zucchini, garlic, basil, salt, and pepper.

ᵒ ᵒ

OLIVES & CAPERS

○ ○

HERE ARE A FEW THINGS TO CONSIDER WHEN ADDING THE "WITH THE SAUCE" INGREDIENTS:

- Extra spices and herbs will enhance the flavors.

- Liquid smoke or smoked paprika will add some smokiness.

- Tomato paste will give the sauce more depth.

- Sugar will help cut the acidity of the tomatoes.

- Capers, olives, or artichokes will give the sauce a tangy punch.

- Cherry or grape tomatoes add fresh, sweet pops of tomato flavor.

- Starchy pasta water will loosen the sauce while also making it adhere to the pasta better.

- Walnuts or sun-dried tomatoes will add some great texture.

- Wilting in some greens will add color and flavor.

○ ○

ZUCCHINI ⋮ GARLIC

Caramelizing onions normally takes a long, long time. I'm talking like an hour or more, just for some onions!? Nuh uh! So I figured out a trick to getting those onions to caramelize in just 10 minutes. It might not be the traditional way, but my hack means you can have a pasta that tastes just like French onion soup on your table in 30 minutes. Now that's a hack I can get behind!

SERVES | 4
TOTAL TIME | 30 minutes
TOTAL COST | Under $3

CHEATER CARAMELIZED ONION PASTA

1. Bring a large pot of water to a boil and cook pasta according to package directions. Set aside ½ cup pasta water before draining the pasta.

2. Heat the oil in a large pot with a lid over medium-high heat. Add the onions, garlic, salt, and sugar. Cover and cook the onions, adjusting the heat as needed to keep them from burning. After 5 minutes covered, the onions should be soft and translucent. Remove the lid and continue to cook to brown the onions, stirring regularly to stop them from burning, about 10 more minutes.

3. Add the cooked pasta, ¼ cup pasta water, and pepper to the pot and toss well to combine. Add the remaining pasta water if needed to help the onions coat the pasta.

14 ounces short pasta, such as penne, shells, or orecchiette (gluten-free if preferred)

2 tablespoons olive oil

4 yellow onions, thinly sliced

2 cloves garlic, minced or pressed

¾ teaspoon salt

½ teaspoon white sugar

½ cup pasta water

¼ teaspoon black pepper

MAKE AHEAD: Store the cooled pasta in an airtight container in the fridge for up to 3 days. You can also freeze the cooled, caramelized onions (before adding the pasta) in an airtight container for up to 3 months.

SERVES | 4

TOTAL TIME | 25 minutes

TOTAL COST | Under $10

I always have a big bowl full of fresh lemons on my counter, and they aren't there just for looks. Lemons make everything better. Plain water? Add lemon! Salad need some zing? Add lemon! Want fluffy pancakes? Add lemon! Have a creamy pasta sauce but it needs just a little more oomph? You guessed it, add lemon! The citrus brightens this creamy sauce, and when the sauce is tossed with hot pasta or gnocchi and wilted greens, you have a delish and simple pasta.

10-INGREDIENT LEMON CREAM PASTA

14 ounces pasta, any shape, or 1 pound gnocchi (gluten-free if preferred)

2 tablespoons vegan butter

2 tablespoons all-purpose flour (gluten-free if preferred)

2½ cups plant-based milk, such as soy or oat

Zest of 4 lemons

Juice of 1 lemon

2 tablespoons finely chopped fresh rosemary or thyme (about 2–4 sprigs, leaves removed from stems)

1 teaspoon salt

¼ teaspoon black pepper

4 cups arugula or baby spinach

1. Bring a large pot of water to a boil and cook the pasta or gnocchi according to package directions.

2. In a large pan over medium-high heat, melt the vegan butter. Once melted, whisk in the flour to form a paste and cook for 1 minute. Slowly whisk in the plant-based milk and keep whisking until completely smooth. Add the lemon zest, lemon juice, rosemary, salt, and pepper and continue to cook until the sauce thickens, about 5 minutes.

3. Add the hot pasta and arugula and toss well so the leaves wilt into the pasta. Serve hot.

QUICK TIP: Anytime you use lemons, zest them first and then save the zest in a small airtight container in the freezer so it will be good to go whenever you need it. Or if you have leftover juice, pour it into an ice cube tray; once frozen, transfer the cubes to a freezer bag or container for later.

MAKE AHEAD: Allow the pasta to cool before storing in an airtight container in the fridge for up to 3 days.

SERVES | 4

TOTAL TIME | 30 minutes

TOTAL COST | Under $10

This is my version of the classic Indian dish, butter chicken . . . but without the butter and without the chicken. Not only was I looking for excellent vegan replacements for both butter and chicken, but after discovering that a lot of traditional recipes require an entire cup (!) of butter and additional cups of heavy cream, I cringed, and knew I wanted to make this one a little healthier too. So, I present you my (mostly) guilt-free version. Ta-da! Not only is it so much healthier, but I daresay it's so much tastier too!

BETTER BUTTER CAULIFLOWER

2 cups white rice or grain of choice

FOR THE SAUCE

2¾ cups water

½ cup raw cashews

1 can (5.5 fluid ounces) tomato paste (about ⅔ cup)

1 tablespoon garam masala

1 teaspoon chili powder

1 teaspoon ground cumin

1 teaspoon salt

½ teaspoon ground ginger

FOR THE BUTTER CAULIFLOWER

2 tablespoons vegan butter

1 yellow onion, chopped

4 cloves garlic, minced

6 cups cauliflower, cut into florets (about ½ large head)

1. Cook the rice according to package directions.

2. For the sauce, add the water, cashews, tomato paste, garam masala, chili powder, cumin, salt, and ginger to a high-powered blender and blend until smooth and creamy. If you do not have a high-powered blender, you may want to soften the cashews first by boiling them in water for 10 minutes, draining, and then adding to the blender with all of the remaining ingredients. This will ensure a smooth sauce.

3. For the butter cauliflower, melt the vegan butter in a large pan or pot over medium-high heat. When melted, add the onions and garlic and sauté until the onions turn translucent and just begin to brown. Pour in the prepared sauce and stir in the cauliflower florets. Cover and bring to a simmer. Stir the cauliflower often so the sauce doesn't burn on the bottom of the pan. Cook until the cauliflower is fork-tender, about 10 minutes. Serve over rice.

MAKE AHEAD: Allow the rice and butter cauliflower to cool completely, then store in separate containers in the fridge for up to 3 days.

SERVES | 4

TOTAL TIME | 20 minutes

TOTAL COST | Under $10

I could drink this sweet ginger-infused sauce, but that might be weird, so instead I decided to pour it over stir-fried broccoli and mushrooms. Good idea. If you're not feeling the broccoli and mushroom vibe, feel free to sub your favorite stir-fry veggies instead. It's all about the sauce in this one!

20-MINUTE STICKY GINGER STIR-FRY

2 cups white rice, preferred grain, or noodles

FOR THE STICKY GINGER SAUCE

1 cup water

6 tablespoons soy sauce (gluten-free if preferred)

¼ cup brown sugar

2 tablespoons rice vinegar

2 tablespoons cornstarch

4 green onions, chopped (set aside some for garnish)

3-inch piece fresh ginger, minced (3 tablespoons)

4 cloves garlic, minced or pressed

FOR THE VEGGIE STIR-FRY

2 tablespoons light oil, such as canola or peanut, plus more if needed

1 head broccoli (12 ounces), cut into florets (about 4 cups)

8 ounces cremini or button mushrooms, quartered

2 teaspoons sesame seeds, for garnish

1. Cook the rice according to package directions.

2. For the sticky ginger sauce, add the water, soy sauce, sugar, rice vinegar, cornstarch, about three-quarters of the green onions (setting aside the rest for garnish), ginger, and garlic to a small saucepan. Cook the sauce over medium-high heat, whisking often, for about 2 minutes, until it begins to thicken. Remove from heat and set aside.

3. For the veggie stir-fry, heat the oil in a skillet over medium-high heat. Add the broccoli and mushrooms and fry, stirring every now and then, until the broccoli is tender and the mushrooms have darkened and reduced in size, 5–10 minutes. Pour the sauce over the vegetables and toss to coat. Serve over the rice, and garnish with the remaining green onions and sesame seeds.

This recipe came about when I was craving a Greek salad but wanted something a little heartier. I ended up tossing the salad ingredients along with a big dollop of hummus and some warmed pita onto a bed of rice, and man-o-man, was I satisfied. It soon became a new favorite easy and healthy weeknight dinner for me.

SERVES | 2 large or 4 small portions
TOTAL TIME | 20 minutes
TOTAL COST | Under $10

GORGEOUS GREEK BOWLS

1. Cook the rice according to package directions.

2. Add the oil, lemon juice, and Greek seasoning to a small jar or bowl. Shake well or whisk to combine.

3. Divide the rice among bowls, then top with cucumbers, tomatoes, olives, onions, hummus, and pita triangles. Drizzle the dressing overtop, as desired, and add salt and pepper to taste.

1 cup white rice (or preferred grain, see Quick Tip)

¼ cup olive oil

¼ cup lemon juice

1 tablespoon Greek Seasoning (page 49 or store-bought)

½ cucumber, chopped (about 1½ cups)

1 large tomato, chopped

½ cup pitted black or kalamata olives

¼ red onion, chopped

½ cup prepared hummus

2 pitas, lightly warmed or toasted, cut into triangles (gluten-free if preferred)

Salt and black pepper, to taste

QUICK TIPS: 1. For a different spin, try subbing brown rice, quinoa, or couscous for the white rice. **2.** If you have leftover dressing, it's perfect for dressing a quick salad or using in a Guzinta Bowl (page 190).

MAKE AHEAD: Bowls can be assembled up to 4 days in advance and kept in the fridge. Store the dressing in a separate container in the fridge for up to 1 week, and then drizzle over the bowls when ready to enjoy.

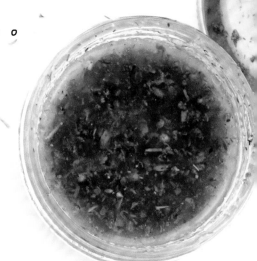

SERVES | 4–6
TOTAL TIME | 25 minutes
TOTAL COST | Under $10

Red lentils are super affordable, very quick to cook, and suck up any flavor you give them, so they are a staple in my kitchen. In this recipe, I spice them up with Mexican-inspired flavors for the most perfect, hearty burrito. I like to stuff my burrito with rice, corn, salsa, and creamy avocado, but feel free to use your favorite fillings instead.

LOADED LENTIL BURRITOS

2 cups white rice

1 tablespoon light oil, such as canola or vegetable

1 yellow onion, finely chopped

2 cloves garlic, minced

4 teaspoons Tacos & More Seasoning (page 48 or store-bought taco seasoning)

2 cups vegetable broth

1 cup red lentils

½ teaspoon salt

4–6 large flour tortillas (gluten-free if preferred)

1 avocado, peeled, pitted, and mashed

½ cup salsa

1 cup fresh or frozen and thawed corn kernels

1. Cook the rice according to package directions.

2. Heat the oil in a pan over medium heat. Add the onions and garlic and sauté for about 5 minutes, until the onions become translucent. Add the taco seasoning and continue to cook for 1 minute more, until fragrant. Add the broth, lentils, and salt, then cover and bring to a low simmer for about 8–10 minutes, until all of the broth has absorbed and the lentils are cooked.

3. Assemble the burritos by filling each tortilla with the rice, lentil mixture, avocados, salsa, and corn. Fold both sides of the tortilla over the filling, then roll from the bottom up so the filling is completely enclosed.

4. Optionally, you can choose to warm the outside of the burrito by placing the assembled burrito, seam side down, in a hot dry pan. Heat for about 1 minute per side, flipping when golden brown on the bottom.

MAKE AHEAD: The rice and lentils can be prepared ahead of time and stored in separate containers in the fridge for up to 4 days. Then just assemble the burritos (following step 3) when ready to enjoy. To freeze, wrap each burrito in parchment paper or plastic wrap then store in an airtight container or freezer bag for up to 3 months. To reheat frozen burritos, microwave unwrapped burritos for 3–5 minutes until heated through.

SERVES | 4
TOTAL TIME | 15 minutes
TOTAL COST | Under $7

It takes only a few minutes to whip up this easy chickpea dish, but it's packed full of sweet barbecue flavor. I love this served over couscous, but it would also be great on rice, quinoa, or even a bun for a messy sloppy-joe-style sandwich.

15-MINUTE PINEAPPLE BBQ CHICKPEAS

1 cup couscous or preferred grain (gluten-free if preferred)

1 tablespoon light oil, such as canola or vegetable

1 yellow onion, chopped

2 cloves garlic, minced

1 can (19 ounces) chickpeas, drained and rinsed (about 2 cups)

1 can (14 ounces) pineapple chunks in juice (about 2 cups, save the juice)

½ cup pineapple juice (leftover from the canned pineapple)

½ cup vegan barbecue sauce

½–1 jalapeño, thinly sliced, for garnish (optional)

2 green onions, sliced, for garnish

1. Prepare the couscous according to package directions.

2. In a large skillet, heat the oil. Add the onions and garlic and sauté for about 5 minutes, until the onions soften and begin to brown.

3. Add the chickpeas, pineapple, pineapple juice, and barbecue sauce. Heat through. Serve over the rice and garnish with jalapeños, if desired, and green onions.

MAKE AHEAD: Store the couscous and prepared pineapple BBQ chickpeas in separate containers in the fridge for up to 4 days.

SERVES | 4

TOTAL TIME | 18 minutes

TOTAL COST | $5–$10
(depending on toppings)

Pizza in about 15 minutes. No, really. My late-night munchies think this recipe is almost too convenient. The cheese-like sauce takes just 5 minutes to whip up. Then, once it's on some pita bread along with my favorite toppings, I can have myself a personal vegan pizza in minutes. Delicious enough to satisfy pizza cravings, small enough that you don't have to share with anyone!

PERSONAL PITA PIZZAS

QUICK TIP: Feel free to use this cheese sauce anywhere else you like as well—on pasta, on nachos, in sandwiches, or in lasagna. It's a simple way to knock a dish up a few levels.

FOR THE CHEESE SAUCE

2 cups plant-based milk, such as soy or oat

¼ cup cornstarch

3 tablespoons nutritional yeast

1 teaspoon salt

½ teaspoon garlic powder

FOR THE PIZZAS

4 pitas (gluten-free if preferred)

1 cup tomato sauce

QUICK TIP: If using sun-dried tomatoes in oil, don't forget to save the leftover oil so that you can make Pizza Popcorn (page 78).

TOPPINGS (CHOOSE 1–4)

Sliced black or green olives

Chopped sun-dried tomatoes (dry or in oil, see Quick Tip)

Fresh basil leaves, sliced

Sliced mushrooms

Red or yellow onion, thinly sliced

Bell peppers, chopped

Pineapple chunks

Jalapeño, thinly sliced

Marinated artichoke hearts, chopped

Arugula

Fresh spinach leaves

Tomato slices

Capers

Olive oil

Barbecue sauce

Nutritional yeast

Crushed red pepper flakes

Dried oregano

Italian Seasoning (page 48 or store-bought)

Salt and black pepper

1. Preheat your oven to 425°F.

2. To make the cheese sauce, add the plant-based milk, cornstarch, nutritional yeast, salt, and garlic powder to a medium pot and whisk well. Set over medium-high heat and cook for about 5 minutes, whisking often until the sauce thickens. Remove from heat and set aside.

3. Place the pitas on a large baking sheet, using two sheets if needed. Spread the pitas with the tomato sauce, followed by the cheese sauce and toppings of choice.

4. Bake for 6–8 minutes, until the pizzas are hot and the pita has reached your desired crispiness. .

TO FREEZE THE PIZZAS

1. Prepare the cheese sauce and assemble the pizzas, as you would in step 3. Stack the pizzas on top of each other, dividing them with parchment paper layered between each pizza, then seal them in a freezer bag and place in the freezer.

2. To cook pizzas from frozen: Preheat your oven to 425°F. Unwrap and place each pizza on a large baking sheet. Bake for 8–12 minutes, until the pizzas are hot all the way through and getting golden on the edges.

ᴐ ᴐ

MAKE AHEAD: You can make the cheese sauce (step 2) ahead of time and store in an airtight container in the fridge for up to 3 days. It may thicken as it cools, so when you're ready to use it, add a splash of water and whisk to thin, if needed. The pizzas should be assembled and baked fresh or frozen for later.

ᴐ ᴐ

recipe continues

TOMATO ARUGULA

MUSHROOM OLIVE

RED PEPPER

SUN-DRIED TOMATO

o o o o o o o o o o o o o o o o o o o o o o o o o o o

SOME OF MY FAVORITE COMBOS

Tomato Arugula: Tomato sauce, cheese sauce, tomato slices, and arugula.

Mushroom Olive: Tomato sauce, cheese sauce, black olives, mushrooms, and crushed red pepper flakes.

Sun-dried Tomato: Tomato sauce, cheese sauce, and sun-dried tomatoes.

Red Pepper: Tomato sauce, cheese sauce, red bell pepper, fresh basil, and dried oregano.

o o o o o o o o o o o o o o o o o o o o o o o o o o o

SERVES | 4

TOTAL TIME | 10 minutes

TOTAL COST | Under $10

Before my partner, Adam, went vegan, one of his favorite meals was a tuna salad sandwich. So early in our relationship, I made him my chickpea salad sandwich from my first cookbook, *Fuss-Free Vegan*, and while he loved it, it didn't quite hit the spot for him. I noticed that artichokes have a flaky texture similar to fish and a lot of briny flavor, so I tried whipping up the sandwich with artichokes instead. Total winner. This tangy, flaky, creamy sandwich filling is perfect piled high on your favorite bread with lettuce and tomato or even as a side dish on its own.

10-MINUTE ARTICHOKE SALAD SANDWICHES

FOR THE ARTICHOKE SALAD

1 can (14 ounces) artichokes in water, drained (not marinated artichokes, about 1⅔ cups)

1 tablespoon vegan mayonnaise

½ teaspoon New Bay Seasoning (page 49 or store-bought alternative)

¼ red onion, chopped

1 stalk celery, chopped

FOR THE SANDWICHES

8 slices bread (gluten-free if preferred)

4 lettuce leaves

1 tomato, sliced

1. Add the artichokes, mayonnaise, seasoning, onions, and celery to a food processor and pulse several times to combine, making sure not to process too much—you want the artichokes to retain some of their texture. If you don't have a food processor, simply chop the artichokes with a knife and mix with the remaining artichoke salad ingredients in a bowl.

2. Divide the artichoke filling evenly among the four slices of bread (or toast). Top with the lettuce, tomato slices, and the remaining slices of bread and enjoy!

MAKE AHEAD: You can prepare the filling (step 1) ahead of time and store in an airtight container in the fridge for 3–4 days, making this a great take-to-work lunch.

I love making this filling ahead of time and having it ready to go when hunger strikes. It's perfect served hot or cold. I like it on fresh, crunchy lettuce, but if you want something a little heartier, try serving this filling over your favorite grain instead.

SERVES | 4
TOTAL TIME | 10 minutes
TOTAL COST | Under $5

10-MINUTE CHICKPEA LETTUCE WRAPS

1. In a large pot or skillet, whisk the water, soy sauce, cornstarch, rice vinegar, agave, garlic, ginger, and Sriracha together. Add the chickpeas and turn the heat to medium-high. Cook for about 5 minutes, stirring often, until the chickpeas are heated through and the sauce has thickened. Remove from the heat.

2. Fill the lettuce leaves with the chickpea mixture, garnish with sesame seeds, and enjoy!

MAKE AHEAD: You can prepare the chickpea mixture (step 1) ahead of time and store in an airtight container in the fridge for 2–4 days. Enjoy cold or reheat and serve with fresh lettuce leaves.

1 cup water

¼ cup soy sauce (gluten-free if preferred)

2 tablespoons cornstarch

2 tablespoons rice vinegar

1 tablespoon agave or brown sugar

3 cloves garlic, minced or pressed

1-inch piece fresh ginger, minced

1 teaspoon Sriracha or similar hot sauce

1 can (19 ounces) chickpeas, drained and rinsed (about 2 cups)

1 head lettuce, such as romaine, iceberg, or butter, leaves separated

1 tablespoon sesame seeds, for garnish

Beans on toast is a classic recipe, but not like this! Creamy, spicy, and smoky, with crunchy bites of celery—this black bean sandwich is a thing of drool-worthy beauty! Not feeling the bread vibes? These black beans are also fantastic on a salad or in a bowl (page 190).

(page 190)

SERVES | 4
TOTAL TIME | 10 minutes
TOTAL COST | Under $7

SMOKY BLACK BEAN SANDWICHES

1. Add the black beans to a medium bowl and use a potato masher or fork to smash the beans until about half of the beans are mashed.

2. Add the celery, onions, mayonnaise, jalapeños (if using), paprika, and salt and stir to combine.

3. Make the sandwiches by dividing the filling evenly among four slices of bread. Top with lettuce and the remaining slices of bread and enjoy!

MAKE AHEAD: You can prepare the filling (steps 1–2) ahead of time and store in an airtight container in the fridge for 3–4 days. Assemble sandwiches when ready to enjoy or pack a lunch for the day.

1 can (19 ounces) black beans, drained and rinsed (about 2 cups)

2 stalks celery, chopped

¼ red onion, finely chopped

2 tablespoons vegan mayonnaise

½–1 jalapeño, minced (optional)

½ teaspoon smoked paprika

¼ teaspoon salt

8 slices bread, optionally toasted (gluten-free if preferred)

4 lettuce leaves

SERVES | 4
TOTAL TIME | 25 minutes
TOTAL COST | Under $5

This has become one of my more popular recipes on my blog. Not only is it easy to prepare, but it's so flavor-packed that it is a weekly go-to for many of my readers. I had to add this Korean-inspired recipe to the book to make absolutely sure it reaches as many people as possible. It's too good to miss!

SWEET KOREAN LENTILS

2 cups white rice or preferred grain (gluten-free if preferred)

FOR THE SAUCE

2 cups water

¼ cup soy sauce (gluten-free if preferred)

2–3 tablespoons brown sugar

2 cloves garlic, minced or pressed

1-inch piece fresh ginger, minced

1 teaspoon sesame oil

½ teaspoon crushed red pepper flakes

FOR THE LENTILS

1 tablespoon light oil, such as canola or vegetable

½ yellow onion, chopped

1 cup red lentils

Chopped green onions and/or sesame seeds, for garnish (optional)

1. Cook the rice according to package directions.

2. In a medium bowl, mix together the water, soy sauce, sugar, garlic, ginger, sesame oil, and red pepper flakes.

3. To make the lentils, heat the oil in a skillet over medium heat, then add the onions and sauté for a few minutes until the onions soften and begin to brown. Add the lentils and the sauce, cover, and bring to a gentle simmer. Cook until the lentils are tender and most of the liquid is absorbed, about 8–10 minutes. To avoid mushy lentils, be careful to cook the lentils gently and not to overcook them.

4. Spoon the lentils over the rice and garnish with the green onions and sesame seeds, if desired.

QUICK TIP: I love using red lentils in my recipes, as they take only 10 minutes to cook, but if you prefer to use green or brown lentils, go for it—just keep in mind that they will take double the cooking time, about 20 minutes.

MAKE AHEAD: Allow to cool, then store the rice and lentils in separate containers in the fridge for up to 4 days. You can also freeze the prepared lentil mixture for up to 6 months, but if you do so, slightly undercook the lentils so that they don't get mushy when reheated.

This surprisingly simple dish is elegant times eight. (That's very elegant.) These creamy mushrooms are somewhere between a main and a soup. Serve with crusty bread and spoon, sip, and munch your way through this yummy mushroom dish. You can also serve this on a big bowl of pasta.

SERVES | 4
TOTAL TIME | 22 minutes
TOTAL COST | Under $10

CREAMY TUSCAN MUSHROOMS

1. Heat the oil in a large skillet over medium-high heat. When the oil is hot, add the mushrooms and cook for about 5–7 minutes, until the mushrooms have darkened in color and begin to release their juices.

2. Add the plant-based milk, nutritional yeast, garlic, Italian seasoning, salt, and pepper. Bring to a simmer and let cook for 2–5 minutes, until the mushrooms are fork-tender. Stir in the spinach and sun-dried tomatoes. When the spinach wilts into the sauce, it's ready to enjoy. Serve with baguette slices for dipping.

QUICK TIP: Cremini and button mushrooms can range a lot in size. I like picking out the smaller ones for this dish to make them bite-size.

MAKE AHEAD: Store the cooled mushroom dish in an airtight container in the fridge for up to 3 days.

2 tablespoons olive oil

12 ounces cremini or button mushrooms, left whole (see Quick Tip)

1½ cups plant-based milk, such as soy or oat

¼ cup nutritional yeast

2 cloves garlic, minced or pressed

1 teaspoon Italian Seasoning (page 48 or store-bought)

½ teaspoon salt

¼ teaspoon black pepper

2 handfuls spinach (about 4 cups)

⅓ cup chopped sun-dried tomatoes (in oil or dry)

1 baguette, sliced (gluten-free if preferred)

SERVES | 4–6

TOTAL TIME | 20 minutes

TOTAL COST | Under $10

The coconut milk in this recipe is thickened with flour and seasoned with onions, garlic, taco seasoning, and salt, and the result is a creamy, sticky, melty, cheesy sauce that tastes amazing—and is perfect in these super quick quesadillas.

QUICKER QUESADILLAS

1 tablespoon light oil, such as canola or vegetable

1 yellow onion, chopped

4 cloves garlic, minced or pressed

¼ cup all-purpose flour (gluten-free if preferred)

1 can (14 fluid ounces) full-fat coconut milk (about 1¾ cups)

1 can (19 ounces) black beans, drained and rinsed (about 2 cups)

1 cup fresh or frozen and thawed corn kernels

1 tablespoon Tacos & More Seasoning (page 48 or store-bought taco seasoning)

1 teaspoon salt

4–6 large tortillas (flour or corn)

½ cup salsa (mild, medium, or spicy), for serving

1. In a large pan or saucepan, heat the oil over medium-high heat. Add the onions and garlic and sauté until the onions turn translucent and begin to brown, about 5 minutes. Sprinkle the flour over the onions and stir to coat. Cook 1 minute more to warm through. Add the coconut milk and stir to combine. Stir in the beans, corn, seasoning, and salt. Cook for another 3–5 minutes, until the mixture cooks into a thickened cheesy sauce.

2. Spoon the filling onto one side of a tortilla. Fold the tortilla in half, making a half circle.

3. Heat a dry large skillet over medium-high heat. When hot, add the folded tortilla to the pan and warm for about 2 minutes on each side, until golden brown. Remove from the pan and cut into triangles. Repeat with the remaining tortillas and filling. Serve hot with salsa.

SERVES | 4

TOTAL TIME | 30 minutes

TOTAL COST | Under $10

Coating tofu in seasoned cornstarch before frying it gives it a crispy, tasty skin. Trust me, once you fry tofu using this method, you won't want to fry it any other way! Just wait, it gets better. The seasoned tofu gets tossed with broccoli in a buttery, herby sauce that will have you licking your lips. Serve this recipe with your favorite grain or over a bowl of hot pasta to make it a hearty meal.

HERB BUTTER TOFU & BROCCOLI

2 cups quinoa or preferred grain (gluten-free grain if preferred)

5 tablespoons cornstarch

1 teaspoon salt

1 teaspoon black pepper

1 block (12 ounces) extra-firm tofu, cut into 1-inch cubes or strips (see Quick Tip)

4 tablespoons vegan butter, divided

1 head broccoli, cut into florets

¼ cup water

6 cloves garlic, sliced

2 teaspoons Italian Seasoning (page 48 or store-bought)

½ cup vegetable broth

1 handful fresh parsley, roughly chopped, for garnish

1. Cook the quinoa according to package directions, and set aside.

2. In a medium bowl, mix together the cornstarch, salt, and pepper. Add the tofu and toss to evenly coat. Set aside.

3. Melt 1 tablespoon of vegan butter in a large non-stick skillet over medium-high heat. Add the broccoli and water and cover with a lid. Simmer for about 3 minutes, until the broccoli is fork-tender but still has some bite. Remove the lid and cook for another 2–3 minutes to brown the broccoli. Remove the broccoli from the pan and set aside.

4. To the hot pan add 2 more tablespoons of vegan butter. Once melted, add the tofu and fry, turning as needed, until the tofu is golden brown on all sides, 5–10 minutes. Remove the tofu from the pan, setting it aside with the broccoli.

5. Add the last tablespoon of vegan butter to the pan, and when melted, add the garlic and Italian seasoning. Cook for about 30 seconds, until the garlic starts to brown. Pour in the broth and use your spoon to scrape up and release any bits stuck to the bottom of the pan. Now return the broccoli and tofu to the pan and toss to coat in the sauce. Garnish with chopped parsley and serve hot with quinoa.

QUICK TIP: While I don't think it's required in this recipe, some people like to press their tofu to remove extra water before cooking it, which can make it a little chewier. To do this, either use a tofu press or wrap the tofu in a clean dish towel and place something flat and heavy on top, such as a cast-iron skillet with a couple of cans of beans. Press it for 15–30 minutes before cutting and cooking.

SERVES | As many as you like

TOTAL TIME | 20 minutes

Whatever's in the fridge, guzinta it! One of the best ways to save money and time when cooking is to use the food that you already have. Use that lingering solo carrot, the remaining salad dressing, and the handful of leftover beans. You can choose to make guzinta bowls as complicated or as simple as you like, with as much or as little of each ingredient as you find appetizing. This recipe is a little different in that I haven't priced out the ingredients or provided specific quantities, and I didn't actually limit it to 10 ingredients. Instead, this guide is intended to help you use up all the leftovers in the fridge so that no food goes to waste.

GUZINTA BOWL GUIDE

QUICK TIP: I always cook up extra grains whenever a recipe calls for them so that I know I can make a Guzinta Bowl later in the week!

PICK YOUR BASE

Cooked white rice

Cooked couscous

Cooked quinoa

Cooked rice noodles

Cooked udon noodles

Cooked ramen noodles

QUICK TIP: If your beans or tofu are unseasoned, you can easily jazz them up by heating them up in a small saucepan with 1–4 tablespoons barbecue sauce. Or heat 1 teaspoon oil with 1 teaspoon spice mix (see page 48), then toss with the tofu or beans.

ADD HEARTINESS (CHOOSE 1-3)

Chickpeas

Black beans

Kidney beans

Lima beans

White beans (such as kidney or navy)

Edamame

Lentils

Smoked tofu

Prepared tofu

 ITALIAN

ADD LEFTOVERS (OPTIONAL)

Tofu from the 20-Minute Breakfast Sandwiches (page 54)

Smoky Black Bean Sandwich filling (page 181)

Legumes from the Sweet Korean Lentils (page 182)

Chickpeas from the 10-Minute Chickpea Lettuce Wraps (page 179)

15-Minute Pineapple BBQ Chickpeas (page 170)

15-Minute Apple Chickpea Salad (page 121)

Lentil filling from the Loaded Lentil Burritos (page 168)

20-Minute Sticky Ginger Stir-Fry (page 164)

Filling from the 10-Minute Artichoke Salad Sandwiches (page 176)

Brisk Broccoli Salad (page 117)

10-Minute Zesty Corn Salad (page 123)

ADD VEGGIES (CHOOSE 2–5)

Leftover cooked vegetables

Cooked greens, such as spinach or kale

Fresh greens, such as romaine, spinach, kale, or arugula

Cooked potatoes or sweet potatoes

Fresh or cooked broccoli or cauliflower

Carrots, grated

Bean sprouts

Avocado, sliced or chopped

Warmed corn kernels, fresh or frozen and thawed

Mushrooms, sliced and sautéed

Bell peppers, sliced

Warmed peas, fresh or frozen and thawed

Baby corns

Cabbage, thinly sliced

Red onions, thinly sliced

Cucumbers, chopped

Beets, grated

Cherry or grape tomatoes, halved

Tomato, cut into wedges

Radishes, thinly sliced

Celery, chopped

Cooked squash

Artichoke hearts

QUICK TIP: You can quickly cook a potato in the microwave by first piercing it all over with a fork to release steam, then microwaving it on high for 5–10 minutes, depending on the size of the potato, until tender all the way through.

recipe continues

THAI

MEXICAN

BBQ

FLAVOR BOOSTERS (CHOOSE 1–3)

Walnuts

Peanuts

Almonds

Sunflower seeds

Pepitas (pumpkin seeds)

Green onions, sliced

Fresh cilantro, roughly chopped

Fresh parsley, roughly chopped

Lime or lemon wedges

Sesame seeds

Poppy seeds

Nutritional yeast

Sun-dried tomatoes

Tortilla chips

Caramelized onions (page 157)

SAUCE IT UP (CHOOSE 1–2)

Barbecue sauce

Tahini

Soy sauce

Salsa

Hot sauce

Sriracha

Lemon juice

Lime juice

Peanut butter

Other nut or seed butter

Balsamic vinegar or glaze

Mustard

Olive oil

Classic hummus

Flavored hummus

Hummamole (page 84)

Guacamole

Mushroom Gravy (page 41)

Loaded Queso Dip (page 94)

Sesame Dressing (page 129)

Maple Dijon Dressing (page 129)

Smoky Lime Dressing (page 130)

Hummus Caesar Dressing (page 130)

Hummus Ranch Dressing (page 130)

Hummus Blue Cheese Dressing (page 130)

Artichoke Dressing (page 131)

Peanut Lime Dressing (page 131)

Avocado Cilantro Sauce (page 131)

---

1. For your bowl to be a success, it's important you stick within a theme so that you don't end up with weird combinations of ingredients. So first assess your fridge and the ingredients you have on hand, then decide on a theme—Mexican, Thai, barbecue, Italian, Mediterranean, etc.

2. Now pick your base and put a large scoop in the bottom of your bowl. You can choose to enjoy the base hot or cold. Follow this with your hearty selections, leftovers, veggies, flavor boosters, and sauces. Make sure you follow your theme as you go so that you end up with a bowl of flavors that complement each other. Then enjoy!

SOME OF MY FAVORITE COMBOS

Mexican: White rice, black beans, smoked tofu, romaine lettuce, corn, salsa, and Avocado Cilantro Sauce (page 131).

Thai: Rice noodles, medium-firm tofu tossed in a splash of soy sauce, edamame, grated carrots, red cabbage, peanuts, green onions, sesame seeds, Peanut Lime Dressing (page 131), and Sriracha.

BBQ: Quinoa, kidney beans simmered in barbecue sauce, cooked sweet potato, cucumbers, sliced bell peppers, caramelized onions, and pepitas.

Italian: Quinoa, lima beans heated with Italian Seasoning (page 48), arugula, sautéed mushrooms, red onions, grape tomatoes, parsley, and balsamic glaze.

Mediterranean: Couscous, chickpeas heated with olive oil and garlic powder, mixed greens, sliced sun-dried tomatoes, chopped walnuts, olives, chopped parsley, lemon juice, and olive oil.

MEDITERRANEAN

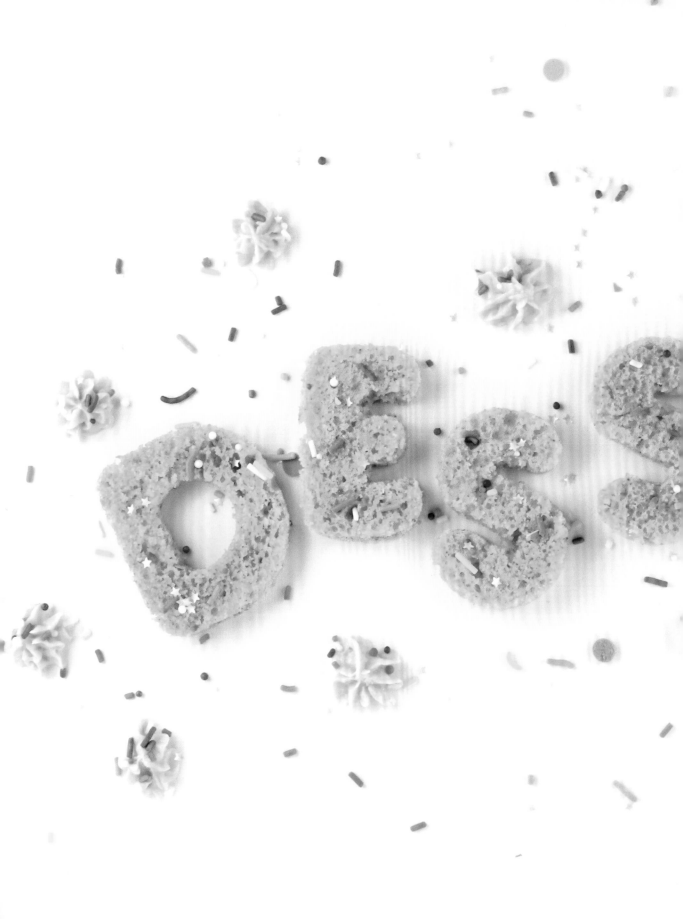

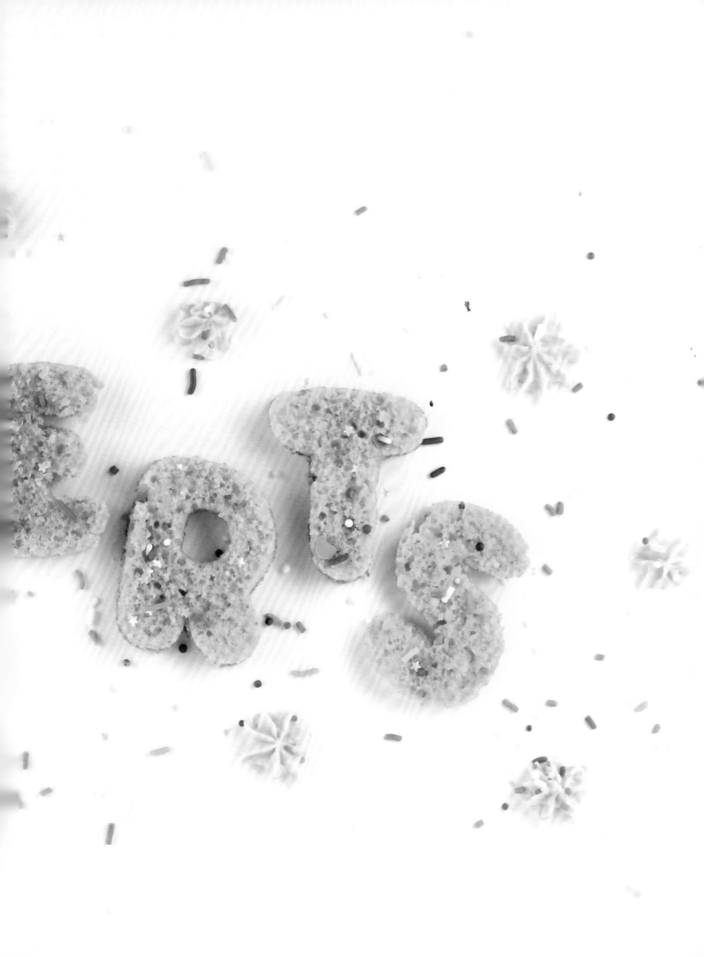

SERVES | 1
TOTAL TIME | 8 minutes
TOTAL COST | Under $1

Individual gooey brownies in a mug in under 10 minutes. Yep, I thought this was a good idea . . . a very good gooey, chocolaty idea. I enjoy spooning at this brownie as is, but it can also be amped up by topping with some vegan ice cream or a drizzle of peanut butter. This recipe makes one brownie in a cup, but feel free to make as many mugfuls as you like.

BROWNIE IN A CUP

3 tablespoons all-purpose flour (gluten-free if preferred)

3 tablespoons brown sugar

3 tablespoons cocoa powder

3 tablespoons light oil, such as canola or vegetable

3 tablespoons water

2 tablespoons vegan chocolate chips

1 tablespoon chopped walnuts (optional)

Scoop of Lickety-Split Ice Cream (page 216, optional)

1. In a large microwave-safe mug, mix together the flour, sugar, cocoa, oil, water, chocolate chips, and walnuts, if using. Microwave on high for 2 minutes, until the brownie looks mostly dry on top and is set. If not set, continue to cook in 10-second increments until it is. Let cool for 5 minutes, then top it with a scoop of vegan ice cream, if desired, and enjoy.

Banana flambé is cool and all, but I prefer not to set my kitchen ceiling on fire. These warm and gooey cinnamon-coated banana slices have all the flavor and none of the danger. They're gorgeous on their own or great on top of vegan ice cream or dairy-free yogurt, served with a splash of coconut cream, or even on peanut butter toast.

SERVES | 2
TOTAL TIME | 11 minutes
TOTAL COST | Under $1

FAST FRIED CINNAMON SUGAR BANANAS

1. In a medium bowl, mix together the sugar and cinnamon. Add the banana slices and gently toss to coat.

2. Melt the vegan butter in a large skillet over medium-high heat. Once melted, add the bananas and fry for 2–3 minutes per side, until lightly golden and warmed through. Enjoy alone or serve with a scoop of vegan ice cream or other addition if desired.

3 tablespoons white sugar

1½ teaspoons cinnamon

2 bananas, sliced into quarters

2 tablespoons vegan butter

Scoop of Lickety-Split Ice Cream (page 216, optional)

MAKES | About 4 chocolate bars
TOTAL TIME | 28 minutes
TOTAL COST | $5–$10
(depending on your choices)

Making homemade chocolate bars is actually so easy and so much fun! Just like my Kitchen Sink Cookies (page 202), these chocolate bars are totally customizable! If one person likes fruit and nuts in their chocolate, while the other likes crispy rice cereal in theirs, well, you know what to do! These pretty bars also make great little gifts.

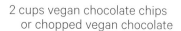

PERSONALIZED CHOCOLATE BARS

2 cups vegan chocolate chips or chopped vegan chocolate

TOPPINGS (CHOOSE 1–3)

4–5 vegan cookies, broken into pieces

1–2 tablespoons vegan-friendly sprinkles

¼ cup rice cereal or corn flakes

¼ cup dried fruit, such as raisins, banana chips, crystalized ginger, or cranberries

¼ cup chopped nuts, such as hazelnuts, almonds, or peanuts

¼ cup vegan candies

¼ teaspoon flake salt or regular salt

1. Line a large baking sheet with parchment paper.

2. Add the chocolate chips to a medium microwave-safe bowl and melt the chocolate, stirring it every 20 seconds. Once it is almost melted (there will still be a few chips left), remove it from the microwave and stir to finish melting. This will ensure you don't burn the chocolate.

3. Pour the chocolate onto the prepared baking sheet and spread with a spatula until the chocolate is about ¼ inch thick. Sprinkle the top with toppings of choice, and lightly pat the toppings into the chocolate, if need be. Chill in the freezer for about 25 minutes, until the chocolate is set, or if you're not in a rush, you can pop the chocolate in the fridge until it's set (it will take a little longer to fully set this way). Once set, you can either break it into pieces or use a large sharp knife (that has been warmed under hot water, then thoroughly dried) to cut it into bars.

MAKE AHEAD: You can store the chocolate bars in an airtight container in your pantry for up to 1 week.

MAKES | 14–16 cookies
TOTAL TIME | 28 minutes
TOTAL COST | Under $5
(not including add-ins)

The other day, I was just about to bake up my chocolate chip cookies when I realized I was completely out of chocolate chips! Way to plan ahead, Sam. I had to improvise, so instead of chocolate chips, I dug around in the cupboard and started pulling out whatever little add-ins I could find. It turns out this was a completely brilliant move, as I came up with so many different delicious cookie flavors, all with the same dough recipe! Salty mini pretzel cookies, chewy dried strawberry cookies, crunchy nut-packed cookies, birthday sprinkle-filled cookies . . . Have fun decorating your cookies with everything but the kitchen sink!

KITCHEN SINK COOKIES

1¾ cups all-purpose flour

½ cup white sugar

½ cup brown sugar

¾ teaspoon baking powder

¼ teaspoon salt

¾ cup vegan butter, softened

3–6 tablespoons plant-based milk, such as soy or oat

1 teaspoon vanilla extract

ADD-INS (CHOOSE UP TO 1½ CUPS OF ANY COMBO)

1 cup crumbled cookies

1 cup slightly crushed salted potato chips

1 cup slightly crushed pretzels

½–1 cup vegan candies

1 vegan chocolate bar, broken into pieces

¾ cup vegan chocolate chips

½ cup vegan-friendly sprinkles

¼ cup coffee beans

1 cup breakfast cereal

1 cup salted popcorn

1 cup nuts

¾ cup shredded coconut

1 cup dried fruit, such as raisins, cranberries, or chopped apricots

1. Preheat your oven to 350°F. Lightly grease a large baking sheet or line with parchment paper.

2. In a large bowl, mix together the flour, white and brown sugars, baking powder, and salt. Add the softened vegan butter, plant-based milk, and vanilla, stirring until a dough is formed.

3. Stir the add-ins into the dough. For larger add-in pieces, such as prepared cookies or broken chocolate bars, you can instead push them into the balls of cookie dough just before baking.

4. Take about 2 tablespoons of cookie dough, roll into a ball, and flatten on the baking sheet. Repeat with remaining dough, spacing the cookies about 3 inches apart. Bake for 14–18 minutes, until they still look almost raw but are lightly golden underneath. This will ensure a chewy cookie. Let cool for 10 minutes before enjoying.

MAKE AHEAD: Store cooled cookies in an airtight container in the pantry for up to 1 week or in the freezer for up to 3 months.

You put the lime in the coconut and mix it all up . . . Or the lemon. Or the orange. Or the grapefruit. They're all delicious! This custard is fresh and creamy all at the same time. I love making different variations of it with whatever citrus I have on hand. Crumbling a gingersnap cookie on top before serving makes it taste similar to a key lime pie—but in a cup!

CITRUS & COCONUT CUSTARD CUPS

1. In a small pot, whisk together the coconut milk, sugar, and cornstarch. Make sure the cornstarch is mixed in well to avoid lumps. Set over medium heat and continue to whisk as the mixture thickens. Cook for about 5 minutes, until the custard is thick enough to coat the back of a spoon. Remove from heat and whisk in the citrus zest and juice. Pour the custard into four small bowls or cups (teacups work well). Chill in the fridge for a minimum of 20 minutes, until chilled all the way through.

2. When ready to serve, either enjoy as they are or crumble a gingersnap overtop each custard just before serving for a layer of added crunch.

1 can (14 fluid ounces) full-fat coconut milk (about 1¾ cups)

½ cup white sugar

2 tablespoons cornstarch

1 tablespoon lemon, lime, orange, or grapefruit zest

¼ cup lemon, lime, orange, or grapefruit juice

4 vegan gingersnap cookies, graham crackers, or vanilla wafers (optional, gluten-free if preferred)

MAKE AHEAD: These will keep, covered, in the fridge for 3–5 days.

This cute little crisp will taste like it was made in your grandma's kitchen, but it's actually made in the microwave in just 5 minutes. Shhhh, don't tell, it's a secret. It's the perfect size for two to share, or for one giant serving for yourself (I don't judge). Enjoy it on its own, or serve it with vanilla Lickety-Split Ice Cream (page 216), a drizzle of coconut cream, or vegan vanilla yogurt.

SERVES | 2
TOTAL TIME | 10 minutes
TOTAL COST | Under $5

10-MINUTE MINI BERRY CRISP

1. Add the oats, flour, sugar, vegan butter, cinnamon, and salt to a bowl and mash together with a fork until the butter is mixed in and you reach a crumbly texture. Stir in the nuts.

2. Add the fruit to a microwave-safe baking dish or bowl about 5 × 5 inches in size. If the fruit is frozen, first microwave the fruit alone for 1 minute on high. If it's fresh, continue on to step 3.

3. Spread the crisp topping over the fruit and cook in the microwave on high for 4–5 minutes, until the berries start bubbling through the crisp topping. Remove from the microwave and allow to cool for 3–5 minutes before serving on its own or with some vegan ice cream.

¼ cup whole rolled oats (gluten-free if preferred)

3 tablespoons all-purpose flour (gluten-free if preferred)

3 tablespoons brown sugar

3 tablespoons cold vegan butter

¼ teaspoon cinnamon

⅛ teaspoon salt

¼ cup chopped walnuts or pecans

2 cups fresh or frozen berries or chopped fruit, such as blueberries, strawberries, raspberries, peaches, apples, etc.

Lickety-Split Ice Cream (page 216, optional)

SERVES | 4
TOTAL TIME | 12 minutes
TOTAL COST | Under $5

When I get delivery Chinese or Thai food, I always seem to be left with an extra tub of rice that I don't want to waste, so I came up with this super simple and super delicious rice pudding. Don't worry, you don't need to wait for delivery to make this recipe; when making a dish from the Mains chapter (page 160) that calls for plain rice, prepare a little extra so you can make this delicious dessert.

LEFTOVER RICE PUDDING

2 cups cooked rice

1 can (14 fluid ounces) full-fat coconut milk (about 1¾ cups)

¼ cup white sugar

¼ teaspoon cinnamon

¼ teaspoon salt

½ cup raisins (optional)

1 teaspoon vanilla extract

1. Mix together the rice, coconut milk, sugar, cinnamon, and salt in a medium pot. Set over medium-high heat and bring to a simmer. Continue to cook at a simmer for about 5–10 minutes, stirring, until the rice pudding has thickened. Stir in the raisins, if using, and vanilla and heat through for another 2 minutes. If the pudding gets too thick, add a splash of plant-based milk or water to thin. Serve hot or cold.

QUICK TIP: I love to use full-fat coconut milk for an extra-rich pudding, but if you're not a fan of coconut, or you don't have it on hand, feel free to use whatever kind of plant-based milk you have. Opt for a plant-based milk higher in fat to keep this pudding creamy.

MAKE AHEAD: You can make the rice pudding ahead of time and store in an airtight container in the fridge for 2–3 days.

SERVES | 4
TOTAL TIME | 30 minutes
TOTAL COST | Under $5

I know it seems weird to put tofu in a dessert, but you gotta trust me on this one. Silken tofu doesn't have much flavor, but it does add light, airy creaminess to this dessert, giving it the perfect luxurious texture. Mix it with sweetener and melted chocolate and the result is somewhere between a pudding and a mousse, with no tofu in sight! Enjoy these chocolate pots alone or top them with fresh berries, shaved chocolate, or a dollop of Coconut Fruit Dip (page 90).

3-INGREDIENT CHOCOLATE POTS

½ cup (3.5 ounces) vegan chocolate chips or chopped vegan chocolate

1 package (10.5 ounces) silken tofu, drained (about 1¼ cups)

¼ cup corn syrup, agave, or maple syrup

1. Melt the chocolate in a microwave-safe bowl in the microwave, stopping to stir it every 20 seconds. Once it is almost melted (there will still be a few chips or small pieces left), remove it from the microwave and stir to finish melting. This will ensure you don't burn the chocolate.

2. Add the tofu and corn syrup to a blender or small food processor and blend until smooth and creamy. Pour in the melted chocolate and blend until incorporated.

3. Spoon the mixture into four ramekins, small bowls, or glasses and chill in the fridge for 25 minutes or until ready to serve.

MAKE AHEAD: These will keep, covered, in the fridge for 3–5 days.

Traditional coconut macaroons require lots of dairy and fussing about to whip the egg whites. They're not vegan and require too much hassle in my opinion. My recipe for coconut macaroons is not only vegan, but so easy, too, using just four ingredients! That's my kinda recipe. Lightly crisp on the outside and chewy in the middle, these are a perfect make-ahead treat or homemade gift.

MAKES | 12 macaroons
TOTAL TIME | 28 minutes
TOTAL COST | Under $3

4-INGREDIENT COCONUT MACAROONS

1. Preheat your oven to 375°F. Line a large baking sheet with parchment paper.

2. In a large bowl, mix all the ingredients together. Use a cookie scoop, mini ice cream scoop, or spoon to form 12 little mounds of the coconut mixture on the prepared baking sheet. Bake for 15–18 minutes, until the tops are lightly browned. Let cool before enjoying.

2 cups sweetened shredded coconut
½ cup full-fat coconut milk
¼ cup cornstarch
1 teaspoon vanilla extract

MAKE AHEAD: Store the cooled macaroons in an airtight container in the fridge or at room temperature for about 1 week, or in the freezer for up to 3 months.

MAKES | 12 turnovers

TOTAL TIME | 30 minutes

TOTAL COST | Under $10

These taste like mini apple pies wrapped in flaky puff pastry! Insert drool emoji here. Unlike pie pastry, puff pastry is surprisingly easy to work with and very forgiving. Even if your unbaked turnovers look pretty wonky, you'll be amazed by how gorgeous they look coming out of the oven. You can easily find prepared puff pastry in the freezer section of your grocery store, and many brands are accidently vegan (usually the cheaper brands, so it's a win-win)! Just check the ingredients to make sure.

EASY AS APPLE... TURNOVERS

2 cups peeled and small diced apples, any kind (about 2 apples)

2 tablespoons brown sugar

¾ teaspoon cinnamon

2 sheets (1 pound) frozen puff pastry, thawed (check to make sure it's vegan)

2–3 tablespoons plant-based milk, such as soy or oat (optional)

2–3 tablespoons white sugar (optional)

1. Preheat your oven to 450°F. Line a large baking sheet with parchment paper.

2. To a medium bowl, add the apples, brown sugar, and cinnamon, and mix to evenly coat the apples.

3. Roll out the puff pastry to about ⅛ inch thick. Use a knife or pizza cutter to cut the dough into twelve 4-inch squares. Fill each square with about 2 heaping tablespoons of apple filling. Fold the pastry in half diagonally over the apples to make a triangle, and use a fork to press and crimp the edges closed. Repeat with the remaining turnovers. Use a sharp knife to cut three slits in the top of each turnover. Carefully transfer to the prepared baking sheet. It's okay if they look a little wonky; they will look beautiful once baked.

4. Optionally, you can brush the top of each turnover with a bit of plant-based milk and then sprinkle sugar over top. This will make the turnover extra golden and sparkly.

5. Bake for 12–15 minutes, until the pastry is puffed up and golden. Let cool on the pan for 10 minutes before serving.

MAKE AHEAD: I love serving these slightly warm from the oven, but leftover turnovers will still be great when stored at room temperature for up to 2 days.

SERVES | 2

TOTAL TIME | 10 minutes
(plus freezing time)

TOTAL COST | Under $1
(for the basic recipe)

If you haven't heard of "nice cream" before or you just haven't perfected how to make it yet, this is the guide for you! When bananas are frozen and blended, they make an almost instant soft-serve-style ice cream, so I always keep a large bag full of peeled and sliced bananas in my freezer so that I can whip up this 5-minute ice cream whenever sweet cravings strike! The banana flavor is mild, so you can enjoy it plain as a vanilla ice cream, or you can add an endless amount of add-ins to make any variety of ice cream you could possibly enjoy! I've listed my favorite recipes here, but feel free to play around and make your own combinations.

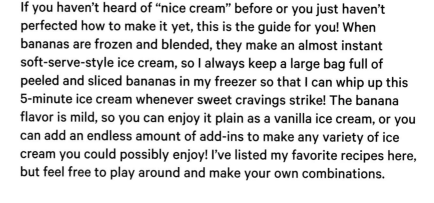

BASIC ICE CREAM

Add the bananas to a food processor or high-powered blender and blend, stopping to scrape the sides as needed, until you reach a smooth consistency. If the ice cream is too thick, add 1 tablespoon at a time of plant-based milk until you reach a completely smooth soft-serve texture. The less plant-based milk you add, the firmer the ice cream will be. You can firm up the ice cream even more by popping it in the freezer for about 20–30 minutes. This ice cream is best enjoyed within a few hours of preparation.

If you plan to make any of the additional flavor options, follow the directions below. Read those instructions first, as there may be a slight variation to this basic recipe.

2 ripe bananas, sliced and frozen solid

¼ cup plant-based milk, such as soy or oat, if needed

1 teaspoon vanilla extract or ¼ vanilla bean, seeds scraped

1 tablespoon corn syrup, maple syrup, or agave

1 batch Basic Ice Cream

VANILLA

Blend the vanilla and corn syrup along with the Basic Ice Cream ingredients, until smooth.

BASIC

CHOCOLATE

CHOCOLATE

Blend the cocoa powder and corn syrup along with the Basic Ice Cream ingredients, until smooth.

2 tablespoons cocoa powder

1 tablespoon corn syrup, maple syrup, or agave

1 batch Basic Ice Cream

DOUBLE CHOCOLATE

Blend the cocoa powder and corn syrup along with the Basic Ice Cream ingredients, until smooth. Add chocolate chips and pulse a few times to mix in.

3 tablespoons cocoa powder

1 tablespoon corn syrup, maple syrup, or agave

1 batch Basic Ice Cream

2 tablespoons vegan chocolate chips

PEANUT BUTTER

Blend the peanut butter along with the Basic Ice Cream ingredients, until smooth.

3 tablespoons smooth or crunchy natural peanut butter, or other nut or seed butter

1 batch Basic Ice Cream

CHOCOLATE PEANUT BUTTER

Blend the cocoa powder and corn syrup along with the Basic Ice Cream ingredients, until smooth. Drizzle in the peanut butter and pulse to swirl.

2 tablespoons cocoa powder

1 tablespoon corn syrup, maple syrup, or agave

1 batch Basic Ice Cream

2 tablespoons smooth natural peanut butter

recipe continues

VANILLA

DOUBLE CHOCOLATE

PEANUT BUTTER

CHOCOLATE PEANUT BUTTER

STRAWBERRY SWIRL

MINT CHOCOLATE CHIP

COOKIES 'N' CREAM

COFFEE

MOCHA

STRAWBERRY SWIRL

Blend the strawberries and vanilla along with the Basic Ice Cream ingredients, until smooth. Add the strawberry jam and pulse to swirl.

1 cup frozen strawberries

½ teaspoon vanilla extract

1 batch Basic Ice Cream

3 tablespoons strawberry jam

MINT CHOCOLATE CHIP

Blend the peppermint extract and food coloring along with the Basic Ice Cream ingredients, until smooth. Add the chocolate chips and pulse a few times to mix in.

⅛ teaspoon peppermint extract

Few drops vegan green food coloring (optional)

1 batch Basic Ice Cream

3 tablespoons vegan chocolate chips

COOKIES 'N' CREAM

Once the Basic Ice Cream ingredients are blended into a smooth ice cream, add the cookies and pulse a few times to mix in.

1 batch Basic Ice Cream

¼ cup crumbled crème-filled chocolate cookies

COFFEE

Blend the espresso powder and corn syrup along with the Basic Ice Cream ingredients, until smooth.

2 teaspoons instant espresso powder

1 tablespoon corn syrup, maple syrup, or agave

1 batch Basic Ice Cream

MOCHA

Blend the cocoa powder, corn syrup, and espresso powder along with the Basic Ice Cream ingredients, until smooth.

3 tablespoons cocoa powder

1 tablespoon corn syrup, maple syrup, or agave

2 teaspoons instant espresso powder

1 batch Basic Ice Cream

recipe continues

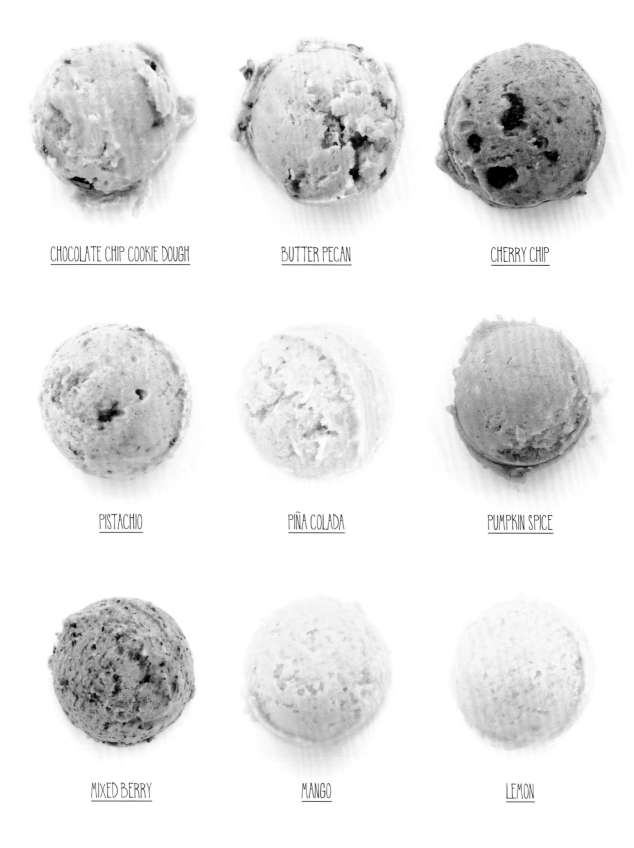

CHOCOLATE CHIP COOKIE DOUGH

BUTTER PECAN

CHERRY CHIP

PISTACHIO

PIÑA COLADA

PUMPKIN SPICE

MIXED BERRY

MANGO

LEMON

CHOCOLATE CHIP COOKIE DOUGH

Blend the vanilla along with the Basic Ice Cream ingredients, until smooth. Add the cookie dough and chocolate chips and pulse a few times to mix in.

½ teaspoon vanilla extract

1 batch Basic Ice Cream

¼ cup Kitchen Sink Cookies dough (page 202), rolled into small balls

2 tablespoons vegan chocolate chips

BUTTER PECAN

Blend the vegan butter, maple syrup, and vanilla along with the Basic Ice Cream ingredients, until smooth. Add the pecans and pulse a few times to mix in.

1 tablespoon vegan butter

1 tablespoon maple syrup or brown sugar

½ teaspoon vanilla extract

1 batch Basic Ice Cream

2 tablespoons chopped pecans

CHERRY CHIP

Blend the cherries, corn syrup, and vanilla along with the Basic Ice Cream ingredients, until smooth. Add the chocolate chips and pulse a few times to mix in.

1 cup frozen pitted cherries

1 tablespoon corn syrup, maple syrup, or agave

½ teaspoon vanilla extract

1 batch Basic Ice Cream

2 tablespoons vegan chocolate chips

PISTACHIO

Blend ¼ cup pistachios and food coloring, if desired, along with the Basic Ice Cream ingredients, until smooth. Add the remaining 2 tablespoons pistachios and pulse a few times to mix in, for texture.

¼ cup + 2 tablespoons raw pistachios, divided

Few drops vegan green food coloring (optional)

1 batch Basic Ice Cream

PIÑA COLADA

Blend the coconut milk and pineapple along with the bananas, until smooth. Add the shredded coconut and pulse a few times to mix in.

¼ cup full-fat coconut milk (sub for the plant-based milk)

1 cup frozen pineapple chunks

2 ripe bananas, sliced and frozen solid

2 tablespoons shredded coconut (sweetened or unsweetened)

recipe continues

¼ cup frozen pumpkin purée

2 tablespoons maple syrup or brown sugar

½ teaspoon Pumpkin Pie Spice (page 49 or store-bought)

1 batch Basic Ice Cream

PUMPKIN SPICE

Blend the pumpkin purée, maple syrup, and pumpkin pie spice along with the Basic Ice Cream ingredients, until smooth.

1 cup mixed frozen berries

1 tablespoon corn syrup, maple syrup, or agave

1 batch Basic Ice Cream

MIXED BERRY

Blend the berries and corn syrup along with the Basic Ice Cream ingredients, until smooth.

1 cup frozen mango chunks

1 tablespoon corn syrup, maple syrup, or agave

1 batch Basic Ice Cream

MANGO

Blend the mangoes and corn syrup along with the Basic Ice Cream ingredients, until smooth.

2 tablespoons lemon juice

1 tablespoon corn syrup, maple syrup, or agave

1 teaspoon lemon zest

1 batch Basic Ice Cream

LEMON

Blend the lemon juice, corn syrup, and lemon zest along with the Basic Ice Cream ingredients, until smooth.

OPTIONAL TOPPINGS

Vegan chocolate syrup · Natural peanut butter (or other nut or seed butter) · Chopped nuts · Crumbled cookies · Broken pretzels · Fresh berries · Fresh banana slices · Shredded coconut · Citrus zest · Sesame seeds · Quick Stovetop Granola (page 63) · Toasted whole rolled oats · Vegan chocolate chips · Shaved vegan dark chocolate · Chopped mint, basil, or rosemary · Vegan-friendly sprinkles · Cool Coconut Fruit Dip (page 90) · Vegan candies · Chopped Easy Peasy Peanut Butter Squares (page 224)

These magic little bars taste like peanut butter cups but better because they are way less fussy to make. You can use crunchy or smooth peanut butter for this recipe, but I prefer crunchy because of the awesome texture it gives these treats.

EASY PEASY PEANUT BUTTER SQUARES

1 cup powdered sugar

6 tablespoons vegan graham cracker crumbs or other vegan cookie crumbs (gluten-free if preferred)

¼ cup chunky or smooth natural peanut butter or other nut or seed butter

¼ cup vegan butter, melted

4 ounces (⅔ cup) dark vegan chocolate or vegan chocolate chips, melted (see Quick Tip)

1. Line an 8 × 4-inch loaf pan (or similar-size dish) with parchment paper.

2. In a medium bowl, mix together the powdered sugar, cookie crumbs, peanut butter, and vegan butter to make a thick dough. Dump the dough into the prepared pan and firmly press down to cover the bottom.

3. Melt the chocolate in a microwave-safe bowl in 20-second increments, stopping to stir as needed. Remove it from the microwave just before it is completely melted (there will be tiny pieces left) and stir to finish the melting. (This will ensure you don't burn the chocolate.) Pour the melted chocolate over the dough base layer and spread evenly.

4. Chill in the freezer for 15–20 minutes, until the chocolate is set. Once set, remove from the pan and cut into 1-inch squares. You can cut the squares when frozen, but they are easiest to cut when they are room temperature, so the chocolate doesn't shatter.

QUICK TIP: These squares are very sweet, so I prefer to use a dark chocolate of 70% or higher to balance the flavors.

MAKE AHEAD: Prepared bars can be stored in an airtight container in the fridge for up to 1 week or in the freezer for up to 3 months.

This is as if a grilled cheese sandwich and a pie had a baby, and that baby tasted good, really good . . . in a totally vegan kind of way. Er . . . Ahem. OK, how about this: This is kind of like having a slice of warm handheld pie, perfect served with a glass of your favorite cold plant-based milk. While you can use any bread to make this sandwich, it really tastes best with a simple white bread—this is not the place to be healthy! Feel free to double or triple as needed to make as many sandwiches as you like!

SERVES | 1
TOTAL TIME | 10 minutes
TOTAL COST | Under $3

EASY AS PIE SANDWICH

1. In a small bowl, mix together the berries and sugar, smashing about half of the berries with your fork while doing so. Let sit for about 5 minutes so the sugar dissolves.

2. Butter one side of each slice of bread.

3. Heat a skillet or pan over medium heat and place one of the slices of bread, butter side down, in the hot pan. Spread the berry mixture over the bread and top with the nuts, chocolate chips, and remaining slice of bread, butter side up. Cook for about 3 minutes, until the bottom is browned, then carefully turn over and cook the other side until the chocolate has melted and the bread is browned. Serve hot.

½ cup fresh or frozen and thawed berries, such as cherries, raspberries, strawberries, blueberries, or a mix

1 tablespoon white sugar

2 teaspoons vegan butter

2 slices bread (gluten-free if preferred)

1 tablespoon chopped almonds, pecans, or walnuts

1 tablespoon vegan chocolate chips

MAKES | About 3½ cups (enough for one 2-layer cake or 24 cupcakes)

TOTAL TIME | 15 minutes

TOTAL COST | Under $5

There are the people who see cake as a vehicle for frosting, and there are the people who leave most of the frosting behind on the plate. I've never understood the latter. While I make sure all of my cake recipes are completely delicious without any toppings at all, it's always fun to zhush it up a little with a swirl of sweet frosting (see Quick Tip). These frostings are super quick to make, but they can also be made ahead of time and stored in the freezer for when frosting cravings strike. When ready to enjoy, just thaw and then spread or pipe as desired!

FREEZER FROSTINGS

½ cup vegan butter

½ cup vegetable shortening

3 cups powdered sugar

1 teaspoon vanilla extract

1–4 tablespoons plant-based milk, such as soy or oat, if needed

VANILLA

Add the butter and shortening to a large bowl and use a mixer or whisk to whip until fluffy. Slowly incorporate the powdered sugar. Mix in the vanilla, then add 1 tablespoon of plant-based milk at a time as needed to reach desired frosting consistency.

½ cup vegan butter

½ cup vegetable shortening

2¾ cups powdered sugar

¼ cup cocoa powder

1 teaspoon vanilla extract

1–4 tablespoons plant-based milk, such as soy or oat, if needed

CHOCOLATE

Add the butter and shortening to a large bowl and use a mixer or whisk to whip until fluffy. Slowly incorporate the powdered sugar and cocoa powder. Mix in the vanilla, then add 1 tablespoon of plant-based milk at a time as needed to reach desired frosting consistency.

PEPPERMINT

Add the butter and shortening to a large bowl and use a mixer or whisk to whip until fluffy. Slowly incorporate the powdered sugar. Mix in the peppermint and vanilla, then add 1 tablespoon of plant-based milk at a time as needed to reach desired frosting consistency. Add a few drops of green food coloring, if desired.

½ cup vegan butter

½ cup vegetable shortening

3 cups powdered sugar

2 teaspoons peppermint extract

1 teaspoon vanilla extract

1–4 tablespoons plant-based milk, such as soy or oat, if needed

A few drops vegan green food coloring (optional)

GINGERBREAD

Add the butter and shortening to a large bowl and use a mixer or whisk to whip until fluffy. Slowly incorporate the powdered sugar. Mix in the molasses, vanilla, and pumpkin pie spice, then add 1 tablespoon of plant-based milk at a time as needed to reach desired frosting consistency.

½ cup vegan butter

½ cup vegetable shortening

3 cups powdered sugar

¼ cup molasses

1 teaspoon vanilla extract

1 teaspoon Pumpkin Pie Spice (page 49 or store-bought)

1–4 tablespoons plant-based milk, such as soy or oat, if needed

CINNAMON CREAM CHEESE

Add the butter and shortening to a large bowl and use a mixer or whisk to whip until fluffy. Slowly incorporate the powdered sugar. Mix in the vinegar, vanilla, lemon juice, and cinnamon, then add 1 tablespoon of plant-based milk at a time as needed to reach desired frosting consistency.

½ cup vegan butter

½ cup vegetable shortening

3 cups powdered sugar

1 tablespoon apple cider vinegar

2 teaspoons vanilla extract

1 teaspoon lemon juice

½ teaspoon cinnamon

1–4 tablespoons plant-based milk, such as soy or oat, if needed

recipe continues

VANILLA

CHOCOLATE

PEPPERMINT

GINGERBREAD

CINNAMON CREAM CHEESE

CHOCOLATE CREAM CHEESE

PEANUT BUTTER

STRAWBERRY

CHOCOLATE CREAM CHEESE

Add the butter and shortening to a large bowl and use a mixer or whisk to whip until fluffy. Slowly incorporate the powdered sugar and cocoa powder. Mix in the vinegar, vanilla, and lemon juice, then add 1 tablespoon of plant-based milk at a time as needed to reach desired frosting consistency.

½ cup vegan butter

½ cup vegetable shortening

2¾ cups powdered sugar

¼ cup cocoa powder

1 tablespoon apple cider vinegar

2 teaspoons vanilla extract

1 teaspoon lemon juice

1–3 tablespoons plant-based milk, such as soy or oat, if needed

PEANUT BUTTER

Add the butter and peanut butter to a large bowl and use a mixer or whisk to whip until fluffy. Slowly incorporate the powdered sugar. Mix in the vanilla, then add 1 tablespoon of plant-based milk at a time as needed to reach desired frosting consistency.

½ cup vegan butter

½ cup peanut butter (use sweetened peanut butter, not the natural kind, which can separate)

3 cups powdered sugar

1 teaspoon vanilla extract

1–4 tablespoons plant-based milk, such as soy or oat, if needed

STRAWBERRY

Add the butter and shortening to a large bowl and use a mixer or whisk to whip until fluffy. Slowly incorporate the powdered sugar. Mix in the jam and vanilla, then add 1 tablespoon of plant-based milk at a time as needed to reach desired frosting consistency.

½ cup vegan butter

½ cup vegetable shortening

3 cups powdered sugar

¼ cup strawberry jam (or sub another flavor of preserve)

1 teaspoon vanilla extract

1–4 tablespoons plant-based milk, such as soy or oat, if needed

QUICK TIP: 1. If using any of these frostings to frost the Yellow Cake (page 42) or Devil's Food Cake (page 44) make sure to let your cake or cupcakes cool completely beforehand. **2.** I like using vegetable shortening because it helps the frosting hold up well at room temperature, but if you prefer you can use all vegan butter. Make sure to keep everything cold, and you may need less or no plant-based milk as the frosting will likely be softer.

THANK YOU

Thank you to the love of my life, Adam, for taste testing every recipe and always giving your honest feedback (whether I liked it or not). For doing way more dishes than was your fair share, and for always making sure my wine glass was full. You're my favorite.

Thank you to my mom, dad, and sister for being the best family a girl could wish for. Your enthusiasm for dinner is what made me become the foodie I am, and your continued support means the world to me!

Thank you to Chickpea dog for cleaning up the floor d'oeuvres . . . when they suited her taste preferences anyway.

Thank you to Robert McCullough, Bhavna Chauhan, Rachel Brown, Kate Sinclair, and the entire team at Appetite by Random House for creating this book with me. What an honor to work with such a fabulous group.

Thank you to my blog readers. It's because of your comments and photos that I fell in love with recipe writing. I wouldn't be where I am today without you.

And thank you to all the home cooks who chose this book to be in their kitchen. I hope your copy gets dog-eared, splattered, tattered, bookmarked, and scribbled on, and becomes well-loved.

Bon appetegan!
Sam Turnbull

INDEX